MY SISTER, GUARD YOUR VEIL;
MY BROTHER, GUARD YOUR EYES

My Sister,
Guard Your Veil;
My Brother,
Guard Your Eyes

UNCENSORED IRANIAN VOICES

LILA AZAM ZANGANEH, *editor*

Beacon Press, Boston

BEACON PRESS
25 Beacon Street
Boston, Massachusetts 02108-2892
www.beacon.org

Beacon Press books
are published under the auspices of
the Unitarian Universalist Association of Congregations.

09 08   8 7 6 5 4

This book is printed on acid-free paper that meets the uncoated paper
ANSI/NISO specifications for permanence as revised in 1992.

Composition by Wilsted & Taylor Publishing Services

Library of Congress Cataloging-in-Publication Data

My sister, guard your veil; my brother, guard your eyes :
uncensored Iranian voices / Lila Azam Zanganeh, editor.
        p. cm.
ISBN 978-0-8070-0463-0 (pbk. : alk. paper)
1. Iran—Intellectual life. 2. Iran—Social conditions.
3. Women—Iran—Social conditions—20th century.
4. Women—Iran—Social conditions—21st century.
I. Azam Zanganeh, Lila.
DS266.M92 2006
305.40955'09045—dc22   2005027496

To my parents,
who taught me to speak up

This generation had no past. Their memory was of a half-articulated desire, something they had never had. It was this lack, their sense of longing for the ordinary, taken-for-granted aspects of life that gave their words a certain luminous quality akin to poetry.

Azar Nafisi, *Reading Lolita in Tehran*

CONTENTS

Whether as a haven of exotic sensuality or a stronghold of fanatic religiosity, Iran has, since ancient times, inflamed the popular imagination. Memories of the millennial dynasties of the shahs echo in the minds of onlookers with the convulsive days of the revolution. In the past months alone, Iran has appeared in the news almost daily: nuclear threats, conservative onslaughts, Islamic clampdowns, mock trials, and political assassinations. Yet there seems to be so little that Americans actually know about Iran, and decade after decade, the misunderstandings live on.

Recently, I was forwarded an e-mail written by a prominent member of the Jewish community in New York. It spoke of me and read: "Let's have Leila on a panel, as a representative of the Arab press." A gracious invitation sent, no doubt, with the best intentions. Alas, it so happens that I am neither Leila nor Arab. But like an overwhelming majority of Americans, this gentleman—who knows I am Iranian—believes that Iran is part of the Arab world by virtue of the fact that it is a Muslim country under the yoke of a staunch Islamist regime. Iran's story, past and present, is at once more intricate and more arcane, "something rich and strange."

Perhaps to a greater extent today than ever before, Iran is a political puzzle. Together with Israel and Turkey, it is one of only three non-Arab countries in the Middle East. Historically, the Persian Empire became the first state to grant protection to the Jews 2,500 years ago—centuries before Arab invasions brought

Islam to the Iranian plateaus. Yet Iran is now the world's single "theocracy," the only "Islamic Republic" of the Middle East (excluding Pakistan from the region proper), a virulently anti-Semitic state and—some say—one of the region's most volatile powder kegs. The intransigent rule of the mullahs coupled with a nascent nuclear capacity seem to constitute a threat not only to Iran's neighbors but to international stability at large.

The country's ruling elite, however, strives to embrace the appearance of a democratic process, notably through the organization of elections in which both men and women are allowed to take part. But any parliamentary motion or presidential decree may be unilaterally vetoed by either the Council of Guardians or the supreme religious leader (both of them unelected), thus turning the system into a sham of democracy. Not to mention the "illiberal," inchoate, and severely dysfunctional legal and judicial infrastructures in place. So Iran teems with make-believe democratic institutions and continues to bewilder Western countries.

At the heart of the profound distrust between Iran and the "West" are several ideological and historical factors. First, there is the Islamic Republic's alleged, and somewhat theatrical, unwillingness to negotiate a lasting dialogue with America and Western Europe. Notoriously, the Iranian government thrives on berating the archdemon America and its egregiously corrupt "Western" value system. An Iranian reformist loves to tell a familiar story—in his country, when the conservatives wish to accuse and demean him, they brand him as "Western-struck," which is only one step beneath the ultimate insult: "Western spy." In this fashion, the very concept of "Western" is cursorily used as an ideological scarecrow against which lay Iranians may measure the Platonic ideals of the Islamic Republic.

But the story, of course, is not that simple. America has done its fair share to infuriate Iran over the years. For one thing, there is that illustrious "axis of evil" petition of faith. Only half a century ago, Americans resolutely supported the regime of Shah Mohammad Reza Pahlavi, a fact that the Islamic Republic will likely never forget. After the demise of the shah, the United States backed Saddam Hussein during the grisly Iran-Iraq war, financed groups of Sunni fundamentalists in the Afghan war against the Soviet Union, and covertly negotiated with the Taliban—Iran's sworn enemy—prior to September 11.

Thus Iran's tainted perception of the United States appears to oddly mirror America's perception of Iran. And the recent political developments in both countries—the neocon frenzy on one side and the presidential vow to return to the "rigid principles of the 1979 Islamic revolution" on the other—though incomparable in nature, have only complicated the geopolitical and emotional maps.

To be sure, in the wake of the landslide victory of the Iranian hard-line presidential candidate in 2005, Westerners who believed in the reformist pledges of Mohammad Khatami and the promise of an enlightened Iran are now faced with a looming nimbus of uncertainty. And too often, their knee-jerk reaction is to consider Iran in Manichean terms. There are those who have blind faith in the country's democratic future and those who dread the noxious seeds of the Islamic Republic. There are those who believe, at times too hastily, that Iran is at core a Western-loving nation that can hardly wait for America to save it from its own bloodthirsty leaders. And there are those who are convinced that Iran, by and large, is a nation of Allah-worshipping, gun-toting terrorists.

In truth, Iranians themselves live in a far more complex and schizophrenic reality, at a surreal crossroads between political Islam and satellite television, massive national oil revenues and searing social inequalities. And if Iran is geopolitically menacing and religiously sclerotic, it is also astonishingly young—more than 50 percent of the country is under the age of twenty-five—and ravenously eager to embrace modernity along with a certain avatar of the American dream. Today, at heart, these young Iranians have forged their own dream, and they are often proud of their culture. Some are genuinely religious and believe in a modern, progressive, and tolerant Islam. Many—while mesmerized by their satellite TVs and American sitcoms—remain skeptical about American values. They are inhabited, at times haunted, by a tantalizing duality: naturally drawn by the appeal of all things Western, they harbor a militant sense of local culture and national pride.

What, then, is this elusive Persian identity? And in the words of the eighteenth-century French philosopher Montesquieu, "How can one be Persian"?

My idea is to answer this question by bringing together a collection of Iranian stories that will lend a "literary" presence, and a common platform, to many of those who play a role, large or small, in the contemporary Iranian adventure. Some have written unorthodox political testimonies, others have broken artistic and cultural taboos. Others still have written tales of feminism and eroticism under the Islamic Republic. With each story, *My Sister, Guard Your Veil; My Brother, Guard Your Eyes* aims to corrode fixed ideas and turn cultural and political clichés on their heads.

For there seems to exist endless misconceptions about Iran, some humorous (think camels), others less so (uncouth, Indiana Jones–caliber barbarians). Doubtless, the Islamic Republic exerts a peculiar sway on the American imagination. Surprisingly, at a time when there is ample talk and trepidation about Iran's military arsenal, at a time when the fears aroused by the September 11 attacks have opened doors to blatant expressions of hostility and racism, Iranians have gained a paradoxical gleam of popularity in this country—and around the world. Shirin Ebadi won the Nobel Peace Prize. Azar Nafisi wrote her unexpected international bestseller, *Reading Lolita in Tehran,* and the artistry of Marjane Satrapi's comic strips was compared to Matisse's etching technique in the pages of the *New York Times.* In Hollywood, the actress Shohreh Aghdashloo became the first Iranian Oscar nominee for her role in *House of Sand and Fog,* a film depicting an Iranian family at odds with its rekindled life in San Francisco.

And of course, Iranian movies such as Abbas Kiarostami's *Taste of Cherry*, which was awarded the Palme d'Or at Cannes, have won lavish critical acclaim in both Europe and America.

There's the rub: on the one hand, the possible Iranian connection with al-Qaeda operatives and Iran's overt support of groups the United States classifies as terrorist organizations— such as Hezbollah in Lebanon and Islamic Jihad in Palestine— have put the Islamic Republic back at the center of the world's political chessboard, all the while increasing a deep-rooted and long-standing suspicion of Iran. On the other hand, however, the thunderous success of books like *Reading Lolita in Tehran* and the consecutive publication of a string of other memoirs by Iranian women reveal a growing and correlated curiosity about the country.

All in all, the gap between the multifaceted realities of Iranian political and cultural life and the simplified image one is often fed by politicians and mainstream media alike remains mind-boggling.

My Sister, Guard Your Veil; My Brother, Guard Your Eyes offers an intimate panorama of the country through variegated stories and essays by some of Iran's most gifted writers and artists. Alongside new voices, numerous well-known Iranian personalities have contributed original pieces to the present collection. Azar Nafisi tells us that literature can be the weapon of choice against the totalitarian thrust of Islamist rulers. Marjane Satrapi highlights, sketches in hand, the most outrageous clichés about Iran and Iranians. Abbas Kiarostami, Iran's celebrated filmmaker, discloses his definition of pornography and narrates the intrinsic Persian alchemy of his cinema. The acutely controversial visual artist Shirin Neshat describes her own private world of women without men. Iran's most prominent philosopher, Daryush Shayegan, offers his modern-day mirror version of Montesquieu's *Persian Letters*. The outspoken actress Shohreh Aghdashloo relays what it took her to break free of Iranian gender stereotypes. Reza Aslan chronicles a trip to Qom, the Rome of mullahs, and uncovers why Iran is not a theocracy but a mullahcracy. Salar Abdoh fleshes out the eerie texture of underground lives in Tehran. Azadeh Moaveni provides a snapshot of sex in the time of mullahs. Negar Azimi presents a color-studded fresco of the subversive contemporary art scene in Tehran. Mehrangiz Kar brings to life the trials and tribulations of feminism under the Islamic Republic. Babak Ebrahimian unfolds the secret of "Iranianness." Gelareh Asayesh explains why she grew up thinking she was white—until she arrived in America. Roya Hakakian reminisces about the happy days of Iranian Jews in Tehran. And then there is that unknown yet resonant voice of a young Iranian woman named Naghmeh Zarbafian—one of Azar Nafisi's former students in Tehran. Her voice exposes the looking-glass world of the Islamic Republic through a deftly seditious analysis of an erotic novel by Milan Kundera, censored out of recognition.

In short, *My Sister, Guard Your Veil; My Brother, Guard Your Eyes* strives to open a series of vibrant perspectives on concealed Iranian realms. And in the vein of the most captivating Persian poet of the twentieth century, Forugh Farrokhzad, I can only hope that these texts, in and of themselves, will act as minute "windows" onto Iran.

Lila Azam Zanganeh

THE STUFF THAT DREAMS ARE MADE OF

Azar Nafisi

The story I want to tell begins at the Tehran airport, decades ago, when at the age of thirteen I was sent away to England to pursue my education. Most friends and relatives who were there on that day will remember that I was very much the spoiled brat, running around the Tehran airport, crying I didn't want to leave. From the moment I was finally captured and placed on the airplane, from the moment the doors were closed on me, the idea of return, of home, of Iran became a constant obsession that colored almost all my waking hours and my dreams. This was my first concrete lesson in the transience and infidelities of life. The only way I could retrieve my lost and elusive Tehran was through my memories and a few books of poetry I had brought with me from home. Throughout the forlorn nights in a damp and gray town called Lancaster, I would creep under the bedcovers, with a hot water bottle to keep me warm, while I opened at random three books I kept by my bedside: Hafiz, Rumi, and a modern female Persian poet, Forugh Farrokhzad. I would read well into the night, a habit I have not given up, going to sleep as the words wrapped themselves around me like aromas from an old spice shop, resurrecting my lost but unforgotten Tehran.

I did not know then that I was already creating a new home, a portable world that no one would ever have the power to take away from me. And I adapted to my new home through reading and revisiting Dickens, Austen, Brontë, and Shakespeare, whom I had met with a thrill of sheer delight on the very first day of school. Later, of course, I would begin to discover America through the same imaginative sorcery—the writing of F. Scott Fitzgerald, Saul Bellow, Mark Twain, Henry James, Philip Roth, Emily Dickinson, William Carlos Williams, and Ralph Ellison.

Yet for decades, whether in England or America, my existence was defined by the idea of return. I imposed my lost Iran on all the moments of my life—even transferring to New Mexico for a semester mainly because its mountains and the shaded colors of its star-filled nights reminded me of my Iran. Late in the summer of 1979, two days after I completed the defense of my dissertation, I was on a plane, first to Paris, then to Tehran.

But as soon as I landed in the Tehran airport, I knew, irrevocably, that home was no longer home. And it is apt, I presume, that home should never feel too much like home—that is, too comfortable or too smug. I always remember Adorno's claim that the "Highest form of morality is to not feel at home in one's own home." So for spurring me to pose myself as a question mark, for altering my sense of home, as for so many other things, I should be grateful to the Islamic Republic of Iran.

There was also another sense in which home was no longer home, not so much because it destabilized and impelled me to search for new definitions, but mainly because it forced its own definitions upon me, thus turning me into an alien entity. A new regime had established itself in the name of my country, my religion, and my traditions, claiming that the way I looked and acted, what I believed in and desired as a human being, a woman, a writer, and a teacher were essentially alien and did not belong to this home.

In the fall of 1979, I was teaching *Huckleberry Finn* and *The Great Gatsby* in spacious classrooms on the second floor of the University of Tehran, without actually realizing the extraordinary irony of our situation: in the yard below, Islamist and leftist students were shouting "Death to America," and a few streets away, the U.S. embassy was under siege by a group of students claiming to "follow the path of the imam." Their imam was Khomeini, and he had waged a war on behalf of Islam against the heathen West and its myriad internal agents. This was not purely a religious war. The fundamentalism he preached was based on the radical Western ideologies of communism and fascism as much as it was on religion. Nor were his targets merely political; with the support of leftist radicals he led a bloody crusade against Western "imperialism": women's and minorities' rights, cultural and individual freedoms. This time, I realized, I had lost my connection to that other home, the America I had learned about in Henry James, Richard Wright, William Faulkner, and Eudora Welty.

In Tehran, the first step the new regime took before implementing a new constitution was to repeal the Family Protection Law which, since 1967, had helped women work outside the home and provided them with substantial rights in their marriage. In its place, the traditional Islamic law, the Sharia, would apply. In one swoop the new rulers had set Iran back nearly a century. Under the new system, the age of marital consent for girls was altered from eighteen to nine. Polygamy was made legal as well as temporary marriages, in which one man could marry as many women as he desired by contract, renting them from five minutes to ninety-nine years. What they named adultery and prostitution became punishable by stoning.

Ayatollah Khomeini justified these actions by claiming that he was in fact restoring women's dignity and rescuing them from the degrading and diabolical ideas that had been thrust upon them by Western imperialists and their agents, who had conspired for decades to destroy Iranian culture and traditions.

In formulating this claim, the Islamic regime not only robbed the Iranian people of their rights, it robbed them of their history. For the true story of modernization in Iran is not that of an outside force imposing alien ideas or—as some opponents of the Islamic regime contend—that of a benevolent shah bestowing rights upon his citizens. From the middle of the nineteenth century, Iran had begun a process of self-questioning and transformation that shook the foundations of both political and religious despotism. In this movement for change, many sectors of the population—intellectuals, minorities, clerics, ordinary people, and enlightened women—actively participated, leading to what is known as the 1906 Constitutional Revolution and the effective implementation of a new constitution based on the Belgian model. Women's courageous struggles for their rights in Iran became the most obvious manifestation of this transformation. Morgan Shuster, an American who had lived in Iran, even stated in his 1912 book, *The Strangling of Persia*: "The Persian women since 1907 had become almost at a bound the most progressive, not to say the most radical, in the world. That this statement upsets the ideas of centuries makes no difference. It is the fact."

By 1979, at the time of the revolution, women were active in all areas of life in Iran. The number of girls attending schools was on the rise. The number of female candidates for universities had increased sevenfold during the first half of the 1970s. Women were encouraged to participate in areas previously closed to them through a quota system that offered preferential treatment to eligible girls. Women were scholars, police officers, judges, pilots, and engineers—present in every field except the clergy. In 1978, 333 out of 1,660 candidates for local councils were women. Twenty-two were elected to the Parliament, two to the Senate. There was one female Cabinet minister, three sub-Cabinet undersecretaries (including the second-highest ranking officials in both the Ministry of Labor and Mines and the Ministry of Industries), one governor, one ambassador, and five mayors.

After the demise of the shah, many women, in denouncing the previous regime, did so demanding more rights, not less. They were advanced enough to seek a more democratic form of governance with rights to political participation. From the very start, when the Islamists attempted to impose their laws against women, there were massive demonstrations, with hundreds of thousands of women pouring into the streets of Tehran protesting against the new laws. When Khomeini announced the imposition of the veil, there were protests in which women took to the streets with the slogans: "Freedom is neither Eastern nor Western; it is global" and "Down with the reactionaries! Tyranny in any form is condemned!" Soon the protests spread, leading to a memorable demonstration in front of the Ministry of Justice, in which an eight-point manifesto was issued. Among other things, the manifesto called for gender equality in all domains of public and private life as well as for the guarantee of fundamental freedoms for both men and women. It also demanded that "the decision over women's clothing, which is determined by custom and the exigencies of geographical location, be left to women."

Women were attacked by the Islamic vigilantes with knives and scissors, and acid was thrown in their faces. Yet they did not surrender, and it was the regime that retreated for a short while. Later, of course, it made the veil mandatory, first in workplaces, then in shops, and finally in the entire public sphere. In order to implement its new laws, the regime devised special vice squads, called the Blood of God, which patrolled the streets of Tehran and other cities on the lookout for any citizen guilty of "moral offense." The guards could raid shopping malls, various public spaces, and even private homes in search of music or videos, alcoholic drinks, sexually mixed parties, and unveiled or improperly veiled women.

The mandatory veil was an attempt to force social uniformity through an assault on individual and religious freedoms, not an act of respect for traditions and culture. By imposing one interpretation of religion upon all its citizens, the Islamic regime deprived them of the freedom to worship their God in the manner they deemed appropriate. Many women who wore the veil, like my own grandmother, had done so because of their religious beliefs; many who had chosen not to wear the veil but considered themselves Muslims, like my mother, were now branded as infidels. The veil no longer represented religion but the state: not only were atheists, Christians, Jews, Baha'is, and peoples of other faiths deprived of their rights, so were the Muslims, who now viewed the veil more as a political symbol than a religious expression of faith. Other freedoms were gradually curtailed: the assault on the freedom of the press was accompanied by censorship of books—including the works of some of the most popular classical and modern Iranian poets and writers—a ban on dancing, female singers, most genres of music, films, and other artistic forms, and systematic attacks against the intellectuals and academics who protested the new means of oppression.

In a Russian adaptation of *Hamlet* distributed in Iran, Ophelia was cut out from most of her scenes; in Sir Laurence Olivier's *Othello,* Desdemona was censored from the greater part of the film and Othello's suicide was also deleted because, the censors reasoned, suicide would depress and demoralize the masses. Apparently, the masses in Iran were quite a strange lot, since they might be far more demoralized by witnessing the death of an imaginary character onscreen than being themselves flogged and stoned to death . . . Female students were reprimanded in schools for laughing out loud or running on the school grounds, for wearing colored shoelaces or friendship bracelets; in the cartoon *Popeye,* Olive Oyl was edited out of nearly every scene because the relationship between the two characters was illicit.

The result was that ordinary Iranian citizens, both men and women, inevitably began to feel the presence and intervention of the state in their most private daily affairs. The state did not merely punish criminals who threatened the lives and safety of the populace; it was there to control the people, to flog and jail them for wearing nail polish, Reebok shoes, or lipstick; it was there to watch over young girls and boys appearing in public. In short, what was attacked and confiscated were the individual and civil rights of the Iranian people.

Ayatollah Khomeini's fatwa against Salman Rushdie years later did not represent a divide between Islam and the West, as some claimed. It was a reaction to the dangers posed by a thriving individual imagination on totalitarian mindsets, which cannot tolerate any form of irony, ambiguity, and irreverence. As Carlos Fuentes stated, the ayatollah had issued a fatwa not just against a writer but also against the democratic form of the novel, which frames a multiplicity of voices—from different and at times opposing perspectives—in a critical exchange where one voice does not destroy and eliminate another. What more dangerous subversion than this democracy of voices? And in that sense, America's extraordinary literary heritage kept reminding me, throughout those years, how heavily genuine democracy depends on what we might call a democratic imagination.

But according to the "guardians of morality" in the Islamic Republic, books such as *Lolita* or *Madame Bovary* were morally corrupt; they set wretched examples for the readers, motivating them to commit immoral acts. Like all totalitarians, they could not differentiate between reality and imagination, so they attempted to impose their own version of truth upon both life and fiction. Yet we do not read *Lolita* to learn more about pedophilia, in the same way that we do not immediately decide to live up in the trees after reading Calvino's *Baron in the Tree*. We do not read in order to turn great works of fiction into simplistic replicas of our own realities, we read for the pure, sensual, and unadulterated pleasure of reading. And if we do so, our reward is the discovery of the many hidden layers within these works that do not merely reflect reality but reveal a spectrum of truths, thus intrinsically going against the grain of totalitarian mindsets.

Quite to the contrary, the ruling elite in Iran imposed the figments of its own imagination upon our lives, our reality. My students could never taste the ordinary pleasures of life—what one of them, Yassi, called the blacklisted details that are so readily available to others—such as the caress of the sun on their skin or the wind in their hair. The simple act of leaving the house every day became a tortuous and guilty lie, because we had to dress ourselves in the mandatory veil and be transformed into the alien image the state had carved for us.

In order to escape and negate the alien image—this mandatory lie that began with our appearances and permeated all aspects of our lives—we needed to re-create ourselves and rescue our confiscated identities. To restore our identities, we had to resist the oppressor through our own creative resources. And we had to do this by refusing to choose the same language as our oppressors. Resistance in Iran had come to mean nonviolent confrontation, both through political demands and through a refusal to comply, an insistence upon the individual's own sense of integrity: demanding respect and recognition whoever we were and refusing to become the figments the regime wished to turn us into.

Inexorably, the same rules that had been fashioned to keep the citizens leashed became, over the course of time, weapons with which Iranians demonstrated their dissent. Because the revolution had turned the streets of Tehran and other cities into cultural war zones, in which agents of the state were searching and punishing citizens not for guns and grenades but for other, far more deadly weapons—a strand of hair, a colored ribbon, trendy sunglasses—the regime had politicized not only a dissident elite but every Iranian individual as well. We were energized, not so much because we were innately political but, rather, in order to preserve our sense of individual integrity as women, writers, and academics—in a word, as ordinary citizens who wished to live their lives.

Less than a decade after Ayatollah Khomeini's death, the enlightened revolutionaries—the former young veterans of war and revolution—were starting to demand more freedoms and political rights. The ayatollah's death had left them alone with their rage, their unfulfilled dreams and unspoken desires. Thus the same former revolutionaries who, in 1979, had anathematized all kinds of modernism and democracy now had to turn inward and question their own ideology. This questioning became all the more urgent since they knew how isolated they had grown among the Iranian population and how fast their revolutionary ideals had lost credibility.

At present, the most powerful forces for change in Iran's social landscape are emanating from women as well as from the younger generation of Iranians, the very children who, the Islamists had hoped, would in time rekindle their parents' long-lost political fervor. The members of this generation, however, refused to comply with the authoritarian rules imposed on them, so the Iranian students have found themselves at the forefront of the struggles for social, cultural, and political freedoms. These youths are well aware of how much their political freedoms are contingent on the preservation of their individual rights and personal spaces. They have defied the morality squads by devising resourceful ways to resist the mandatory dress codes, by holding hands, laughing out loud, and watching forbidden films. In the first years of the new century, it is the morality squads that have retreated from the streets of Tehran. And in some ways, it is ironic that many young Iranians, that is, the children of those who once railed against *Gatsby,* have turned to reading Heinrich Böll, Milan Kundera, and F. Scott Fitzgerald, alongside Hannah Arendt and Karl Popper.

I have often asked myself, in fact, how it is that under the worst political and social conditions, during war and revolution, in jails and concentration camps, most victims turn toward works of imagination . . . I remember, almost a decade ago, listening to a former student who was newly released from jail. She told me about how she and one of her cell mates, another former student named Razieh, kept their spirits up by exchanging stories about their class discussions and the books they had read, from Henry James to F. Scott Fitzgerald. My student informed me at the end of her story that Razieh had not been as lucky as she—Razieh had been executed shortly before my other student's release from jail. Since then, I have been haunted by the idea of places where these beloved works of fiction travel, from libraries and classrooms to the dark cells of executioners. We know that fiction does not save us from the tortures and brutalities of tyrannical regimes or from the banalities and cruelties of life itself. James, Razieh's beloved author, did not rescue her from death; yet there is a sense of triumph in the choice Razieh made when all choices seemed to have been taken away from her. Like so many before her, Razieh still preserved her right to choose her own attitude toward a ruthless and undeserved death. She refused to acknowledge the inhumanity and degradation imposed on her by her executioners through remembering and reliving the most joyous experiences of her life. Faced with death, she celebrated what lent life dignity and meaning, what appealed most to her sense of beauty, memory, harmony, and originality—namely, a great work of the imagination. Her own portable world.

You might feel that such works acquire added significance in a country deprived of its basic freedoms, but that they do not matter much here, in a free and democratic country. How relevant are Fitzgerald, Twain, and Flannery O'Connor, you might ask, to our lives in the Western world?

I would respond simply with a passage from *Huckleberry Finn,* in which Huck contemplates whether or not he should give up Jim. Huck knows that, had he gone to Sunday school, "they'd a learnt you there that people that acts as I'd been"—letting a slave go free—"goes to ever lasting fire." Yet his heart rebels against the threats of these "moral" authorities. He sees Jim before his mind's eye in "day and nighttime, sometimes moonlight, sometimes storms, and we a floating along, talking and singing and laughing. But somehow I couldn't seem to strike no places to harden me against him, but only the other kind." So when he remembers Jim's friendship and warmth and imagines him not as a slave but a human being, he decides: "All right, then, I'll go to hell."

In American fiction, Huck has many unlikely fellow travelers: the gentle and genteel women of Henry James, the restless and haunted women of Zora Neale Hurston and Toni Morrison, the dreamers, like Fitzgerald's Gatsby—and all of them decide they would rather give up heaven and risk hell in order to follow the dictates of their hearts and conscience. They each combine a heartrending blend of courage and vulnerability that defies glib answers, smug formulas, and simplistic solutions. How many of us today would give up Sunday school heaven for the kind of hell that Huck ultimately elects for himself?

As Saul Bellow reminds us in *The Dean's December,* a culture that has lost its poetry and its soul is a culture that faces death. And death does not always come in the image of totalitarian rulers who belong to distant countries; it lives among us, in different guises, not as an enemy but as a friend. To mistake sound bites for deep thought, politics for ethics, reality shows for creative entertainment; to forget the value of dreams; to lose the ability to imagine a violent death in Darfur, Afghanistan, or Iraq; to contemplate murder as passing news: are these not indications that now—more than ever—we need the courage and integrity, the faith, vision, and dreams that these books instilled in us? Is this not a good time to worry with Bellow's hero about what will happen if our country loses its poetry and soul?

And we need to write about this. We need to recount what happens to us and to others when we strive to save ourselves from despair, to remind ourselves that tyrants of all stripes cannot confiscate what we value most. The zealots may come in many garbs; they may rail and kill and mutilate in the name of progress or God. But they cannot rob us of our ideals. They cannot steal away our elemental humanity.

Calvino once said, "We can liberate ourselves only if we liberate others, for this is the sine qua non of one's own liberation. There must be fidelity to a goal, and purity of heart, values fundamental to salvation and triumph." And then he added a simple sentence, which, for me, summarizes everything: "There must also be beauty."

It is in just such notions—in a purely human insistence on beauty, in our reveling in ideas, in the storied details of who we are, what we fear, what we wish for—that the imagination thrives.

Too often we conclude that we are practical creatures, essentially political animals. But in us, there is a far greater impulse —a longing for what I will bluntly call the universal. And it is in this leap toward middle ground that we move closer to what effectively binds us: culture, stories, language. For it is here, in what I like to call the Republic of the Imagination, that we are most humane.

I GREW UP THINKING
I WAS WHITE

Gelareh Asayesh

I grew up thinking I was white. When I moved from Iran to America, I discovered otherwise. It took me a while to get the message. I was fourteen when we came to this country. In my twenties, I began a career as a newspaper reporter. One afternoon, I sat in an office in suburban Maryland, telling a black attorney about a Louis Farrakhan speech I'd covered a few nights back. Sitting in that cavernous, brightly lit hall, watching hundreds of black Americans applaud a message that seemed radical to me, I felt that I had stumbled into a parallel universe. "I was the only white person there," I told Wayne. He looked at me as if I'd let him down. "Well, Gelareh," he said. "I don't consider you white."

I was dismayed. But I was also pleased. After all, he was claiming me. "I'm Iranian," I temporized. It was a different story a decade later, when I heard the same words from a white friend. Our daughters were in kindergarten together in St. Petersburg, Florida. We were meeting several other moms at a local fern bar to talk about school. A lamp suspended from the ceiling cast a yellow glow over the table. The restaurant was noisy and dim. As we perched awkwardly on high stools, I mentioned that our principal was concerned about the dearth of nonwhite parents on the school council. State law required diversity. Julie looked at me. "You're not white," she said.

An uneasy silence descended on the table. Julie looked self-conscious. After a moment, we returned to criticizing the physical education program. When the meeting was over, Julie and I exchanged cordial good-byes. Even so, I never felt the same about her. Not just because she challenged my self-perception but because she saw me as a color first, a person second.

It was an experience that felt new no matter how often it was repeated. Growing up in Iran, I was often described as *sabzeh*— olive-skinned. But I never felt disenfranchised by the cultural emphasis on fair skin. My status was determined by other factors: how attractive I appeared, what I wore, where I lived, and whether I'd ever traveled to the West.

In America, status was tallied differently. In my North Carolina high school, I observed that black boys responded to me when white boys didn't. In college, I learned to see myself as a dark-browed, dark-eyed, dark-skinned creature. As a reporter, I discovered that I was well received in the inner city. A newsroom secretary at my first job lamented that she couldn't get credit for me as a minority because I was not a citizen.

Realigning myself to the view of society at large was clearly a matter not only of self-protection but of self-advancement. Yet I could not bring myself to relinquish the racial framework of a lifetime. I was astonished when an Iranian friend, more assimilated than I, told me she was going to march in a rally on behalf of persons of color. "You don't consider yourself a person of color?" Lilly exclaimed. "No," I said, my tone defiant. She didn't say anything more. She didn't have to.

A few years ago, during an expansive night of conversation in Cambridge, Massachusetts, a black writer I'd just met tried to help me articulate my discomfort. "You feel racialized," he said.

"Yes," I said, relieved. I liked the idea that American notions of race were the problem. But in my heart of hearts, I knew the truth was less benign. If Iran was a color-blind society, it was because almost everyone was the same color. Prejudice was perforce organized differently, along economic, religious, and ethnic lines. To acknowledge this is to lay bare my own racism, internalized during all those childhood years of identifying with Americans and Europeans while looking down on Arabs and

Jews, Pakistanis and Indians, Turks, Kurds, Afghans, and—in the rare instances when I met any—blacks. I was no more color blind than Julie of the fern bar. If I was having trouble making the transition from one racial framework to another, it was not because I was above the fray but because I did not want to relinquish the privileges accorded me in one framework and denied me in the other. What passed for white in Iran was colored in America; and I didn't like being demoted.

In Iran, we worship, slogans notwithstanding, the *khareji,* the outsider. By this word we mean not the Afghans, Arabs, Pakistanis, and Turks who are our neighbors but the white Americans and Europeans who have held sway in the region since the Ottoman Empire. Growing up, I envied friends who ordered their clothes from the Spiegel catalogue. At school, a classmate with an Irish mother ranked as minor aristocracy. I was jealous when my cousins were sent to school in England. The whole family was agog when Caroline, an American friend, came to stay with us in Tehran.

Unlike other Americans we knew, Caroline was uncomfortable with her elevated status. Once she walked into a government office to transact some business. The Iranians in the waiting room, expecting her to jump to the head of the line, looked on with resignation and resentment. *Befarma'eed,* Caroline said in accented Farsi. "After you." Decades later, I failed to follow her example. My American husband and I were in Isfahan with our two children when my son developed an eye infection. A friend prominent in the city sent us to a pediatrician he knew. Our hearts sank when we walked into the packed waiting room, but the doctor came out instantly and ushered us into her office. Forestalling complaint, she said loudly: "They're from America." The angry looks vanished, replaced by curious, self-conscious glances, tinged with wistfulness and awe.

I also recall a relative of mine explicating the inherent superiority of the West. A doctor, he was inordinately proud of his brief tenure in Germany during his youth. "You see, a German doctor, he comes in the house, and he leaves his shoes neatly by the door," he told me. "An Iranian, he kicks them off and leaves them where they are." I assume he spoke metaphorically—as a rule, Germans don't leave their shoes outside the door but tramp in residues of whatever they've been walking in. On another occasion, he commended my young daughter's placidity, convinced it was due to my husband's American blood—in his mind, only Iranian babies fussed and squalled. His audience of assorted other relatives nodded wisely in agreement. There was no doubt in their minds that my half-American child was superior to an Iranian one.

The original settlers of the Persian plateau were Aryan tribes —the root of the word "Iran." Iranians consider themselves kin to those orderly Germans, and therefore white. In the West, the word "Aryan," associated as it is with Hitler and hate groups, is hardly a recommendation. In Iran, it is something altogether different, a coveted invitation to the planetary country club. This tenuous link to the global ruling class permits Iranians to look down on the other peoples of the Middle East, most notably the Arabs, who had the temerity to defeat the faltering Persian Empire in the seventh century. Never mind that all those invaders undoubtedly copulated with their new subjects and that the idea of a purebred Persian in Iran today is as absurd as the notion of a blooded Saxon in England. Why quibble when the goal is to have someone to be superior to?

The pecking order in Iran has to do with first world and third world, with West and East. Even so, its subtext is purely racial. The water fountains in the oil fields of Abadan read "Not for Iranians" instead of "Colored Only," but if the lexicon of supremacy had a thesaurus, the two phrases would be listed together. My father, on a business trip to South Africa, discovered yet another synonym: "honorary white." In the months after September 11, an Iranian friend was less fortunate. The anonymous letter in his mailbox called him a "sand nigger" and labeled his blue-eyed, fair-skinned American wife a whore. A few years ago, before the Twin Towers fell, I sat on a plane from Tehran to London and listened to another fair-skinned American lamenting common attitudes to her marriage to an Iranian. "They almost consider it biracial," she said.

I moved from Iran to America in 1977, just before the hostage crisis. For years, I attributed some people's acute awareness of my coloring to this event. Only recently have I realized that for many Americans, being from the Middle East is an issue of race, not of nationality or religion. If it is couched in terms of religion, that is because for most Westerners, Islam is inseparable from race. If Islam had originated among Danes rather than Arabs, would it be seen as it is today: dark, like me, and utterly threatening? Does the Christian faith of killers of abortion doctors, or white supremacists, infuse the religion as a whole with an aura of malice?

Not long ago, a Dutch friend of mine commented that she didn't care to live in Holland any longer—too many Muslims there. She caught the expression on my face and looked self-conscious. "You're not Muslim, are you?" I had to tell her that I was. Years back in Maryland, during the first gulf war, another cordial conversation ground into silence when the police department secretary I was chatting with said: "You know, it says in the Bible those people over there are descended from jackals." I don't know why I bothered to deny it.

For a time, I developed a halfhearted interest in establishing my racial credentials. I looked in encyclopedias, studied census categories, and queried experts, seeking evidence for the national conviction that Iranians are the same race as Germans. I wanted to be able to refute the waitress who, in the process of bringing me a cup of Lipton in my favorite diner, asked, "Is your husband white?"

But all I learned was that both Arabs and Jews are Semites. Whenever I had to fill out a form describing my children's race, I wavered in the grip of deep uncertainty. Depending on the status of my inner dialogue, I might describe my children as "Caucasian" or as "Other." The fact that they belonged in none of the usual categories: black, Hispanic, or Native American, surely supported my notion that Iranians' racial status was TBA.

Eventually, it dawned on me that the people fixating on my

race don't really care whether I'm black, brown, or purple. What matters to them is that I am not white. In America (and Canada, England, or France, for that matter) there are really just two races, white and nonwhite. What is most relevant about me in the eyes of some—though certainly not all—of the people I work, play, and live with is not what I am but what I am not. Most of us retain an ability to appreciate each other as individuals and regard each other with respect, admiration, even affection. But at some preprogrammed level, we remain ever conscious of otherness. In times of doubt, it becomes all too easy to interpret actions through this distorting prism. "You're always late," a close friend complained to me years ago. "I realize it's probably cultural."

I remembered that incident recently, when a black acquaintance failed to show up at a meeting for the second time in a row. "I swear, I think it's cultural," I groused to one of the other attendees. I felt my own smallness even as I spoke the words, but some stubborn part of me refused to take them back. It was easier to believe them, to assign a known cause, even a spurious one, to this disruption of my day. It was easier to yield to the universal need to categorize and file away life's messy quotidian incidents.

Everyone knows the broad outlines of the ladder of prejudice. White is on top, brown in the middle, black at the bottom. Any point of similarity to the white Caucasian at the top of the ladder offers an advantage: a blue-eyed Iranian, for example, is superior to one with dark eyes; an Iranian educated in America is the master of the Iranian educated in his home country. My National Public Radio accent takes me further than my parents' voices, laden with inflections from a faraway land. The options may be limited when it comes to skin color, but it is possible to improve one's status in other ways. I think of it as race laundering: the right clothes, the right car, the right neighborhood can help compensate for that fundamental imperfection: nonwhiteness. I have spent nearly three decades in this country. I shed my accent long ago, and my misfit clothes followed soon thereafter. More difficult to negotiate were the social and cultural idioms. It is easy enough to mimic them—witness my young cousins who, within a year or so of emigrating from Iran, were proving they belonged by injudicious use of the word "man." But mimicry is not the same as assimilation, which takes far longer and offers a chance at coming full circle. For me, it took the imprimatur of American culture at its best to counteract the sense of inferiority that is epidemic in the postcolonial world. I am never so American as when I take pride in being Iranian.

In the 1980s, while this transformation was still incomplete, my aunt visited me from Iran. For the trip, she replaced her black chador with a long tunic, pants, and a scarf in sober hues. But walking amid the marble and bright lights of an upscale mall in Maryland, she drew the eye of everyone who passed. I longed to walk ahead, dissociating myself from this proof of my otherness. To claim her was to lose the social status it had taken me years to acquire. Only love—and shame—persuaded me to reach for her hand. I held it firmly in mine—but avoided eye contact with the people we passed.

Nowadays, I am more likely to put my heritage on parade, using my command of the language, my nice clothes, my palpable affluence to perform an alchemy of sorts—turning a liability into an asset. I perform it most often in the service of my children, whose friends envy their ability to speak Farsi, the Iranian coins they collect on their trips abroad, the colorful native clothes we truck out on special occasions. I went on a field trip to a nearby theater with my daughter's fourth-grade class recently and taught a particularly squirmy boy the odd Farsi phrase. Soon other classmates wanted to learn how to say *Saket* instead of "Be quiet." After the performance, my daughter greeted me with angry tears. "Farsi is private," she said. What she meant was that it is a privilege.

I take a childish pride in my powers of transmutation. But they are provisional, wholly dependent on others. Nothing brings this home like a visit to Iran. In 1992, I traveled to the provincial Iranian town of Ahwaz in the oil-rich deserts bordering Iraq. I was employed by an oil services company to write a story on the status of Iran's postwar oil industry. A company representative, a white European man, arrived in Ahwaz on the same flight. We were to be chauffeured to the same destination— a company house in the city. In the baggage claim area of the small terminal, I saw him standing in the middle of teeming crowds of sunburned, rustic Iranians: the women in flowing black veils, the men in rough-spun coats and baggy pants. He stood half a head taller than everyone else, dressed in a sports coat and open-necked shirt, staring into the distance as he awaited the flunkeys who would deliver him from the smell of dust and sweat and ripe toilets, the babble of voices rising in Farsi and Arabic, the peering dark eyes. I spoke to him in English, seeking acknowledgment as a refugee from his own world.

He did not appear to have heard me. I stood awkwardly by in my stylish scarf and jacket, as invisible to him as my compatriots. Even in the car, he would not meet my eyes. It was only when we were inside the house, and I was completely shorn of my Iranian trappings, sporting Gap and J. Crew clothes, speaking casually of newspaper headlines and Bill Clinton's recent election, that my bona fides were established. We chatted over nonalcoholic beer and potato chips, and he looked at me with awareness and interest, lifting from me that mantle of invisibility.

That night, as I lay awake in my unfamiliar bed, my heart was heavy. I knew that in winning him over, I had betrayed myself.

HOW CAN ONE BE PERSIAN?

Marjane Satrapi

We are set—stuck, really—somewhere between Scheherazade's famed *One Thousand and One Nights* and the bearded terrorist with his manic wife disguised as a crow. By way of flattery, we are told that we are *Persians* and that *Persia* was a great empire. Otherwise, we are Iranians. The Persians are in Montesquieu's writings, in Delacroix's paintings, and they smoke opium with Victor Hugo. As for the Iranians, they take Americans hostages, they detonate bombs, and they're pissed at the West. They were discovered after the 1979 revolution.

To begin with, let it be remembered that Persia is the Greek terminology for Iran. The Greeks chose this name for our country because, when Greece became a powerful nation, Iran was ruled by the Achaemenids, who were "Persians" since they dwelled in the region of Persis. But Iran, for the last four thousand years and for all Iranians, has always been Iran. And it was actually Reza Shah, the last shah's father, who in 1935 requested that every European refer to our country by its real name—Iran.

I left my country for the first time in 1984, never to return up to now, twenty-one years later; since then, prejudices and clichés about Iran have never failed to astonish me.

It can be quite funny sometimes—like in 1995, when I was a student in Strasbourg and a girl in my class ran to me and said, "Come here, I want to show you something you've never seen before!" I followed her, of course, candidly enthusiastic and generous as she was. When we arrived in the schoolyard she

exclaimed, "Look!" I looked—didn't see anything. Since it was February and the temperature was pretty low, I cast a quick glance around everything there was to see before hurrying back inside.

Nothing! At least nothing unusual.

She understood. "Look! It snowed! It's so beautiful—SNOW!" She stressed the word "SNOW," so that I could fully grasp what it was. "Have you ever seen SNOW?"

I told her that Iran was a high-altitude plateau in the western part of Asia, and that it snowed there quite a lot in the wintertime. I also wanted to explain that we had ski resorts thirty miles from Tehran, but I figured it wasn't necessary to remind her how pathetic her two inches of half-melted SNOW were. I also figured she'd probably seen *Not without My Daughter* with all her girlfriends and her entire family, and it wasn't her fault if she thought Iran was nothing but a big desert . . .

"But—Iran's not in Asia!" she said. "Iran's in the East," she added in a deeply confident tone.

The East. That word, I think, is the key to all myths.

Where is it, this legendary East of our fantasies and dreams and hatreds? If you'll admit that the earth is round, then you're always east or west of someone else. And even if you won't go by these silly looking-glass games, even if you wish to base your observations on Greenwich, then why aren't Australia and New Zealand a part of it, too? So the East is not really a geographical fact. And maybe the term "Eastern countries" has more to do with a religious definition—maybe what we really mean is that they're Muslim countries. In that case, is Bosnia an Eastern country? But then again, even if Bosnia were located further east, what in the world does the expression "Muslim countries" mean, anyway? This notion would take us from Bosnia to Somalia, and from Morocco all the way to Indonesia—and such countries are to be found on three continents: Europe, Africa, and Asia. Is that to say that Saudi Arabia and Malaysia share the same culture?

Talking about "Muslim countries" means, in the end, that the one and only factor defining the culture of a given society is religion. That is one factor, indeed—but it is certainly not the only one. Talking about "Muslim countries" also means shrinking dozens of countries down to one single abstract concept . . . so as to better classify them.

Now, of course, should it be suddenly discovered that these countries are as different from one another as Peru and Iceland or France and the United States of America (which, by the way, are four Christian countries), it would become rather tricky to plan exhibitions of Muslim artists—those events that throw together a Turk, an Iranian, and a Syrian, notwithstanding the fact that those three speak three different languages of three different origins to begin with. "Muslim countries" means as little as "Christian countries."

But that's not the worst. The worst is how "Muslim" is defined. What is a Muslim? Unfortunately, the West equates him or her with Bin Laden, that is, with the most radical of all wretched ideas.

The West turns the Muslim into an enemy.

And Iran is a Muslim country.

Thanks to people like the filmmaker Abbas Kiarostami, the writer Azar Nafisi, and the Nobel Laureate for Peace Shirin Ebadi, the image of Iran has been transformed a bit. But how? From Iranian movies, it has been inferred that Iran was a picturesque country where children ran around looking for "the house of their friend." When Shirin Ebadi was awarded the Nobel Prize, the one detail that was immediately noted was that she didn't wear the veil—which was used in France as an argument to hastily pass the law banning the veil...

Iran has extremists, for sure.

Iran has Scheherazade as well.

But first and foremost, Iran has an actual identity, an actual history—and above all, actual people, like me.

FROM HERE TO MULLAHCRACY

Reza Aslan

At least once a month, my cousin Afshin drives a carload of British or German tourists from Iran's sprawling capital, Tehran, to one of the country's many tourist destinations—either the glorious, lyrical city of Shiraz, the ancient ruins of Persepolis, or the palatial gardens of Isfahan. Few people ask him, as I have done, for a ride to Qom, the religious capital of Iran. The very name of the city makes Afshin squirm. He suggests a trip to Mashhad instead.

"Why not visit Imam Reza?" he says, referring to that city's patron saint.

I remind him that his brother, Saleh, lives in Qom and that he would be happy to see us. Afshin grunts, starts the ignition, and pulls onto the dry desert highway, reluctantly heading south toward Qom. It is a scorching morning; the heat rising from the asphalt casts an eerie nimbus on the road before us.

I can't blame Afshin for not wanting to go to Qom. It is difficult to describe the anger and contempt that most Tehranis feel toward the clerical regime. In Tehran the word *akhoond*—Persian for "cleric" or "mullah"—is a swearword. One might say to someone acting in a shady or despicable manner: "Don't be such an *akhoond*!" Before the revolution, clerics were pushed to the head of the line in grocery stores and given the best seats in restaurants. Now, people push roughly past clerics in stores, whispering obscenities; a cleric enters a restaurant in Tehran and one can practically hear the *hiss* rising from the tables. There was a time when a taxi would be emptied so a cleric could ride comfortably. These days, a taxi is almost as likely to run a cleric over than pick him up.

But Qom is a city crawling with clerics, confident and in control of the country. For centuries this dusty provincial town and its famed Feyziyeh Seminary have served as the "Vatican" of Shiism. The Ayatollah Khomeini studied in Qom, as did Iraq's Grand Ayatollah Ali al-Sistani. In fact, nearly every Shiite cleric in the world has at one time or another passed through the hallowed gates of the Feyziyeh to be taught the traditional Shiite sciences: Quranic exegesis, Islamic jurisprudence, philosophy, rhetoric, and theology. What they do not teach in Qom, however, is politics, or economics, or government administration, or international affairs, which is odd, since Qom's graduates no longer run just Iran's mosques and *madresehs* (religious schools); they now run Iran.

Too often, Iran's baffling, bipolar government is dismissed as a "theocracy." But Iran is actually not a theocracy. A theocracy suggests rule by God, and as any Iranian will tell you, God is noticeably absent in Iran. In a theocracy, particularly an Islamic theocracy like Saudi Arabia or Afghanistan under the Taliban, the Quran is the only constitution. Yet the Islamic Republic is constructed upon a remarkably modern and surprisingly enlightened constitutional framework in which are enshrined fundamental freedoms of speech, religion, education, and peaceful assembly. Iran's constitution calls for equality under the law with regard to race, ethnicity, language, and even gender. It provides for a comprehensive amendment process as well as the opportunity to launch national referendums to decide the course of the country. Most importantly, Iran's constitution stipulates that all domestic affairs must be administered "on the basis of public opinion expressed by means of elections," thus establishing an empowered legislature and a strong, independent executive. All of this exists under the moral guidance of a single clerical authority—the *faqih*—who is appointed by an "assembly of experts" based in Qom, which, in turn, is directly elected by the people (if no single religious authority is qualified for the post, then the assembly chooses a "Supreme Court" of three to five clerics).

In theory, the faqih was intended to be a papal figure who would ensure the "Islamic character" of the state. However, in the chaotic aftermath of the revolution, the parameters of the office were dramatically altered as Iran's powerful clerical establishment—helmed by the overwhelming charisma of Iran's first faqih, the Ayatollah Ruhollah Khomeini (who himself invented the post)—put into effect a series of constitutional amendments and judicial rulings that spectacularly extended the scope of its power. The clerics relied on their command of personal militias and extensive numbers of Orwellian subcommittees to wrest control of the provisional government from the hands of the capable, if rather dour, technocrats who had been appointed to lead Iran after the fall of the shah. By the time Saddam Hussein invaded in 1980, the time for debate and dissent over the nature of the republic was over. What had begun as a vibrant experiment in Islamic democracy quickly deteriorated into an authoritarian quagmire—a state ruled by an inept clerical oligarchy with absolute religious and political power. Qom is the heart of that power.

Afshin and I arrive in Qom during the noon prayers. The streets are deserted, save for a few late stragglers shuffling into the mammoth Hazrat Massoumeh mosque anchored in the center of town. The shops encircling the mosque are shut and bolted. There is an expectant stillness in the air. Not even the gray- and white-flecked pigeons waddling across the plaza emit a sound. It is as though the mosque has inhaled the city into itself in a long, bated breath. A few moments later, a rumble echoes through the square, and all at once a mass of worshippers is exhaled onto the streets. The city bursts to life. Suddenly Qom appears like any other college town: overrun with cheap, bustling restaurants, open-air markets, and dark, smoky coffee shops where students are crammed in every nook . . . Except these students are clad in the elegant dark robes and regal turbans of clerical privilege.

Afshin parks the car and together we make our way through the bustling streets toward the Feyziyeh. The school is usually closed to visitors, but Saleh, who is a cleric and teacher here, meets us at the gates and escorts us inside. Right away, I can tell Afshin is uncomfortable. He resents seeing Saleh in his clerical garb. He'd rather imagine his brother dressed in the drab slacks and uncollared shirts they liked to wear so long ago, when they were Marxists on the front lines of a promising revolution that sought to rid Iran of the loathed regime of Mohammad Reza Shah.

These days, there is a tendency, both in the West and in Iran, to view the revolution of 1979 as an *Islamic* revolution instigated at the behest of the Ayatollah Khomeini. This is a historical fiction that emerged out of two and a half decades of postrevolutionary propaganda. The truth is, there were dozens of voices raised against the shah; Khomeini's was merely the loudest. In fact, a full 10 percent of Iran's population actively took part in the overthrow of the shah, thus making it the largest popular revolution in modern history. Feminists, communists, socialists, Marxists, secular democrats, Westernized intellectuals, traditional *bazaari* merchants, die-hard nationalists, religious fundamentalists, Muslims, Christians, Jews, men, women, and children: nearly every sector of Iranian society was represented in the revolution. Khomeini's genius was his intuition that in a country steeped in the faith and culture of Shiism, only the symbols and metaphors of Shiite Islam could provide a collective language with which to mobilize a disparate coalition that had little in common save its virulent hatred of the shah.

By the time the shah was ousted and the Islamic Republic was born, both Afshin and Saleh had been lured away from their Marxist roots by Khomeini's mystifying Shiite populism. In the 1980s, Saleh entered the Feyziyeh spurred by the dream of establishing a new kind of nation—one both democratic and Islamic, both quintessentially Muslim and uniquely Iranian—while Afshin fought on the front lines of the battle against Saddam Hussein to ensure that dream would survive. In the 1990s, Afshin and

Saleh were brought together again, this time as leaders in the energizing reform movement that gripped Tehran in the wake of the stunning 1997 presidential election of Muhammad Khatami, whose goal was to unearth the democratic principles of the constitution that had been blithely ignored for more than a decade. But Khatami proved unable (some say unwilling) to propel the reform movement to its fruition. He withdrew his support, allowing the movement to disintegrate under mass arrests, torture, and murder. The reform movement fractured, and Afshin and Saleh went their separate ways. Saleh returned to the Feyziyeh to fight for democracy from within the system; Afshin now claims that the system itself is the problem and must be abandoned.

Inside Saleh's cramped apartment, the three of us sit on a thick Persian rug, well worn from centuries of students crouching at the feet of their teachers to exchange questions and answers in an ancient Socratic method that has served as the foundation of Shiite training for generations. We sip tea through sugar cubes lodged between our teeth, and I ask Saleh to explain the theory behind clerical rule.

"There are many ways to get from Tehran to Qom," he says. "We could take a car, a bus, a plane, or we could walk. But the cleric is the one who has spent a lifetime studying the map. He has taken the trip many times. He knows with certainty which is the best way. And if he declares 'by plane,' then everyone follows him."

"But if I choose to walk, won't I still get to Qom?" I ask.

"Of course. However, the path will be longer and more arduous."

"And if two clerics differ on the best path, which one is right?"

"Technically the senior-most cleric—the one who has taken the trip most often. But really, they are both right. It is up to you and me to decide which one to follow."

And therein lies the central paradox of the Islamic Republic. Shiism is a religion founded upon open debate and rational discourse. In its nearly fourteen hundred years of history, no Shiite cleric has ever enjoyed unconditional authority over another Shiite cleric of equal learning. Nor has any cleric ever held sole interpretive powers over the meaning of the faith. The Shia have always been free to follow the cleric of their choice, which is in part why Shiism has blossomed into such a wonderfully eclectic faith. It is also why the majority of Shia both inside and outside Iran no longer view the Islamic Republic as the paradigm of the Shiite state, but rather as its corruption.

In truth, the Islamic Republic is neither Islamic nor a republic. It can be described neither as a theocracy nor as a democracy. Iran is something else entirely. It is a "mullahcracy," a bizarre hybrid of religious and third world fascism that, like the fascisms of the past century, has turned into an embarrassing example of populism gone awry.

Before rising to leave, I ask Saleh one final question. "Is this the Islamic Republic you had dreamed of? Is this what you fought for?"

Saleh shoots a quick glance at Afshin before stretching his gentle, bearded face into a gloomy half smile. "No." He shakes his head. "This is something else entirely. I can't even remember what happened to that dream."

DEATH OF A MANNEQUIN

Mehrangiz Kar

I can never forget the day in Tehran when a few extra inches were added to the short skirts of mannequins in the shop windows. I witnessed with my own eyes armed officials entering a clothes shop. With their guns, they pointed to the naked leg of a female mannequin and stared into the frightened face of the shop owner. That day, I felt like these armed officials were scratching their sharp claws against the most intimate surface of my own femininity. And yet because of such attacks—which were taking place frequently in cities throughout the country—shop owners began to systematically direct all their anger and frustration at the helpless mannequins. They threw the mannequins in storage rooms or locked them up in dark, foreboding attics. This treatment of the mannequins is how I first came to realize that the feminine identity of Iranian women was being violated. The excuse, of course, was the need to protect Islamic laws and revolutionary principles.

It was 1979. Within a few weeks, the mannequins were lined up in the shops with their elongated skirts. Fear was wriggling in their lifeless eyes. Pedestrians, still wearing short skirts, would stop at the windows and laugh at this sudden transformation. I even overheard a stylish young girl whisper to her friend: "They are not powerful enough to make us change our style—that is why they have made the mannequins look more Islamic...," and she laughed a triumphant laugh.

In reality, these female mannequins—these inanimate women

—were the reporters of the changes that were transpiring in our lives. As a young woman who had received a political and criminal law degree from Tehran University, as a curious journalist and a member of the Iranian Bar Association, I was particularly interested in observing the effects of these political measures on our everyday lives. The mannequins and the alterations in their appearance became my passion during the very hard and lonely years of the revolution. I felt united with these dolls. The mannequins somehow accurately reflected the systematic aggression against our individual identities. I would talk to these dolls, and I duly wrote down what was happening in their lives. These notes gradually turned into the tale of a series of events that would define the nature, helplessness, and resistance of women under the stormlike attacks that were carried out against them.

The story began when, having deposed the shah's regime, religious leaders insisted on the necessity of women donning the Islamic veil. Meanwhile, these leaders barred female judges from exercising their profession and repealed the Family Protection Act, which guaranteed women the freedom to work, travel, and divorce at will. This provoked anger and rebelliousness among women, even though, in those early years, not all Iranian women were united in the quest for regaining their rights.

Enforcing the Islamic veil as compulsory attire was the most significant step in a succession of laws against women in the first years of the revolution. Before this happened women dressed freely and, in Tehran and other major Iranian cities, many women even followed Western fashion. Both veiled and unveiled women enjoyed a peaceful life; both were respected for their beliefs. The unveiled women were not socially restricted, and they were required to wear the veil only when entering mosques or other holy places. Young girls and women could appear with or without the veil in educational centers and workplaces. Thus it was this unwritten agreement—which was compatible with every principle of international human rights—that was broken in a historic moment.

Women who were not wont to wear the veil did not immediately follow the orders of the leaders of the Islamic revolution. It was a few years before we accepted it—and then we did so essentially out of fear. The female mannequins were the first group of unveiled women in Iran who were forced to wear the Islamic veil. And these mannequins slowly made us realize that the social and political history of our country was being turned on its head.

In the beginning, however, the overnight changes in the mannequins' outfits had not appeared portentous enough to compel Iranian women to wear the veil. So splashing acid on the face and bare skin of women's bodies became a practice of the regime. The print media—which wasn't yet the target of the newly established "governmental censoring centers"—started to inform Iranians of these violent incidents. The shadow of fear had already stolen the glow of hope from countless young girls and women. Iranian women were gradually feeling that, in the eyes of the new regime, they were nothing but lifeless objects with no agency of their own: objects that official and unofficial authorities could invade day and night. The ruling fundamentalists, in effect, considered the individual identity of women as the most perilous threat to their enduring power. Accordingly, they needed to destroy that identity so that their rule would last for centuries to come.

Rumors spread rapidly. Some women believed that the regime's brutal restrictions were merely reactions to the shah's policies of hastening Western-style reforms in the previous years. Others warned that unveiled women had simply become a tool the authorities used to conjure an atmosphere of fear, with the pretext of protecting women's chastity. Such policies, many whispered, were preparing the nation for further repression against the opponents and critics of the Islamists. Meanwhile, the mannequins—who knew nothing of the government's strategic plans to enforce the veil—were still attracting customers with their alluring hair and curvaceous bodies.

The war between Iran and Iraq broke out in 1980. This war targeted Iranian women's identities just as the Islamic revolution had. Young boys were drafted and required to write their testaments before they left for the front. After their martyrdom, the authorities would publish these testaments—in nearly all of them, the martyrs had ordered women to observe the Islamic veil. Their orders turned to slogans and were inscribed on the walls of cities. They read: "My sister, your veil is even more powerful than my blood. Signature: the martyr."

The atmosphere in Iran was one of terror and ruthless oppression. The revolution and the war washed away all the gleeful colors of our lives. Mannequins grew bald, leaving their luscious hair behind in storage rooms. Women, in turn, hid their hair under the imposed Islamic veil. Mannequins had resisted for months before losing their free-flowing hair; for a while, they had even tried to content the martyrs by wearing small triangular headscarves. But those small scarves were not enough. The officials—claiming to protect the martyrs' blood—sat in their SUVs and established the "mobile Islamic moral courts." These mobile courts would destroy unveiled female mannequins and detain women. Their officials would tear apart the unveiled mannequins and force women to lie down on torture beds to be whipped with dozens of lashes for not wearing the proper Islamic garb.

Iranian feminism has grown from the scars of these lashes on women's bodies. It is deeply rooted in the suffocated screams of Iranian women throughout the years. And as a result, the fundamentalists have now begun to dread the feminist explosion that is well on its way.

After the hair was lost, only the roundness of women's faces, their daintily colored lips, their blushing cheeks, and their adorned eyelashes remained visible. But the authorities could no longer tolerate these attractive faces, so they continued the Islamization of women's looks, with a little help from the mannequins. These mannequins were turned into role models for Iranian women: they were already veiled, but this wasn't enough. Tradesmen, alarmed by the drastic repression, took action in accordance with the new Islamic orders. Gradually, the color of the mannequins' faces faded away. The rouge of their lipstick and their blush evaporated. Their eyes started to appear dead and hollow. A sense of fright nested in their gaze that bore little resemblance to the air of modesty and chastity the Islamic Republic wished to summon. It did not take long for these mannequins to adopt the role of leaders of the repressed women. Ironically, as we morphed into Islamic-looking women, we obeyed a bunch of lifeless dolls. New values were being measured on their bodies first. The shop owners were constantly reducing and severing femininity, in keeping with orders. Mannequins had lost their main raison d'être to become sheer religious and political instruments. The sparkle of cheerfulness had fled their style. The enthusiasm for interacting with the opposite sex was waning among the people. Any attempts to look attractive brought about a sense of sinful dread and guilt. The colors black, brown, dark blue, and gray had conquered the world, it seemed—although among its glum siblings, red had managed to survive as the symbol of the martyrs' blood. It was the messenger of the repressive orders and reminded women of the lack of charm and bliss in their lives.

On the surface, it was as though modernity had given in to religious tradition. Foreign observers flocked to Iran with journalist visas, exploring the religious centers of political power and the depressed atmosphere of the cities. They were the reporters of the darkness and sorrow that weighed on the transformation of Iranian society. They introduced Iranian women to the world as masses of Islamic-looking shadows represented by the color black. Journalists from all over the world were reporting the Islamic government's aggressive methods and its projects for the separation of the sexes in careers and educations. And for fear of the regime, people never let these reporters into their private gatherings. Thus for many years, the world remained unaware of the conflicting public and private mores in Iran. They believed that Iranians had detached themselves from music, dance, singing, happiness, and their individual identities. They had no idea what was going on behind closed doors. The lifeless mannequins and sad pedestrians became the customary targets of cameras. A fictitious image of Iranian women was introduced to foreign eyes.

The owners of the clothes shops finally came to the conclusion that they might be better off detaching the heads of the mannequins from their bodies altogether. The authorities were claiming that the lips of women were aphrodisiac and their eyes stimulating. The shop owners were confused and did not know what to do to save their businesses from the attacks of the regime. So all of a sudden, they cut the heads off their mannequins. A diagonal surface replaced the necks of these beheaded dolls, on which the owners had now thrown long and dark scarves. Their spongy breasts were slashed from their bodies. Instead, the owners installed two little coils on the empty spots, so that the "feminine gender" might modestly be suggested beneath the ample Islamic garments. The coils displayed the mutilated gender of the mannequins.

These beheaded mannequins were left with only a round face made out of cardboard. They had no eyes, no eyebrows, no noses, no mouths. The ideal woman for fundamentalists was a woman who did not have eyes to see, a tongue to speak, and legs to run away. The shop owners then chopped off the fingers of the female mannequins and replaced their hands with narrow, extended plastic cylinders. Thus they once and for all obliterated every aspect of feminine identity and appearance: lush hair, groomed nails, coal-black eyes, suggestive glances, and scarlet lips.

For many years, foreign journalists never knew that liberty, the pursuit of happiness, modernity, entertainment, and even interactions with the opposite sex existed under the cold and repressed surface of the cities. It took two decades for the world to learn about the schizophrenic existence of the people of Iran, and especially about the resistance of Iranian women. The schizophrenic lifestyle in Iran then became world news. People in Tehran and other cities began to voluntarily invite foreign journalists to their private gatherings. Slowly, the notion of feminism, which had not been fully assimilated by Iranian society, managed to sashay its way through the tortuous labyrinth of the regime. Feminism thrived under women's chadors and their imposed Islamic garments. It surreptitiously grew strong. Women learned the secrets of defending their individual identities. They confounded the enforced values and created their own fashion out of the Islamic veil. Garments were cut shorter and their colors shifted to brighter tones. In 2005, dark pink was high fashion in Iran. And the material of Islamic clothing is now more delicate than it ever was.

These changes have taken as long as twenty-six years to occur. But women's needs and demands are not met, evidently, by merely tailoring shorter, tighter, brighter, or softer garments. To this day, Iranian women have continued to be severely harmed by the regime through sexual discrimination and violent punishments such as detainment, flogging, mutilation of hands and feet, and stoning to death.

In Iran's official language, Farsi, there is no actual word for "feminism." And a group of Iranian sociologists claims that, of approximately 30 million women who live in Iran, a total of 29 million have never heard the word "feminism" in any other language either. The circulation of books with feminist content does not exceed two thousand copies, and on International Women's Day, in March of 2005, only about two thousand women attended a public gathering. No matter—although only tacitly, feminism has now begun to define itself in the individual and social behavior of Iranian women in their everyday lives. So much so that Islamic fundamentalists have become quite helpless in bridling feministic tendencies and seem unable to restrict the feminist demands of their own wives, daughters, and sisters.

The signs of this social agitation are apparent in the country's national statistics. More than 60 percent of applicants currently admitted to universities are women. At the same time, the rates of divorce and "fornication"—which is considered a crime in Iran—are rapidly increasing. The rate of marriage has steadily decreased over the years, and the soaring incidence of prostitution and female drug addiction has caused enormous distress among fundamentalists.

Today, both religious and nonreligious women are bent on regaining their individual identity and freedom. Those who adhere to the principle of a religious government are striving to unearth feminist concepts in Islamic texts. And those who are advocates of the separation of religion and state parade their feminine identity using Western symbols and social attitudes. They also tirelessly fight to keep their lives private and out of sight of governmental agents. Overall, these two groups of women have inched closer to their ultimate goals throughout the years. They criticize the current situation and claim their rights. They express their dissatisfaction through individual and collective reactions to the regime, without much heeding its threats.

In 2005, precisely on International Women's Day, a symbolic assembly of Iranian women announced its demand for changes in the Islamic constitution as its first effort to regain stifled rights. The demand, in and of itself, was significant, demonstrating that Iranian women are willing to publicly tear apart the layer of religious tradition that oppresses them. In fact, their presence in the unofficial job market as vendors, cashiers, waitresses, operators in cab services, real estate dealers, owners of convenience stores and other shops is increasing. Inflation and high prices, the rising number of single mothers, and the lack of social protection have incited women to join the job market and have thus noticeably modified the masculine appearance of Iran's cities.

My belief is that that it won't be long until the day Middle Eastern women are stirred by a new women's movement—one that has risen from the land of Iran, from the pain, sorrow, and bruises of our revolution. My belief is that it won't be long until our mannequins start looking, once again, like our sulfurously modern mannequins of times past.

THE LAST CHAPTER IN THE BOOK OF EXODUS

Roya Hakakian

If another Book of Exodus were to be written, the departure of Jews from Iran would make up its last chapter. I've often wondered what it was that prompted my father to sell our house, his dream home, located in one of Tehran's trendiest neighborhoods, at #3 Alley of the Distinguished, and leave for the United States. That house was a monument to his success. The son of a traveling fabric salesman had made good: left the village, educated himself, and settled in the heart of the capital. Our house was where all the extended family gathered for Passover every year. To honor the ancient Israelites' hasty departure from Egypt, we hastened ourselves, rallying around my mother, waging our own crusade. Our enemies were not in the least alike: the slaves had fought against Pharaoh, whereas we fought against dirt. Yet a feeling of urgency descended upon #3 Alley of the Distinguished. We armed ourselves, as modestly as our ancestors, with an arsenal of brooms, rags, mops, scrubs, and sprays.

We awoke at dawn, when the "cotton beater" made his yearly visit. He camped in the corner of the courtyard, stripped our quilts and mattresses, and removed all the cotton inside. Then, squatting among the loose cotton, he brought out a harplike tool. Inserting it in the heap, he plucked at the coarse strings till the flattened cotton, caught in the strings, separated and regained its fluffiness. The muffled notes of his tool rose in the air. Those notes and the white cloud that surrounded him were all that we heard or saw of him till dusk.

Inside the house, we got busy. We brought down the curtains, dusted every rod, rolled every rug, and swept underneath everything. Searching our closets, we emptied our wallets and handbags, unrolled our pant cuffs, lined up every jacket and pair of trousers on the clothesline, and turned the pockets inside out. We stretched the corner of a rag over our index fingers, tracing along the sides of each drawer to its four corners and twirling our fingertips around a few times. The merriment would come later, only when seriousness had been paid its due.

For those three weeks, we attached biblical meaning to any tiny deviation from the ordinary routine of our household. In the holiday microcosm that formed in our kitchen, we spotted signs of the divine. The Red Sea flowed at the foot of our thawing refrigerator. Golden shafts of light, emanating from its open door, parted the gloomy fluorescence of the kitchen. The gas burner, which we wheeled out of storage, became our occasional burning bush. In a vat over it, we boiled water and dipped perfectly clean dishes to scald away any trace of the nonkosher for Passover foods, while our savior, our seasonal Moses, our year-round Job, Mother, with an outstretched arm, lamenting her migraine, led us in our epic battle against dirt.

Despite the chores, we enjoyed Passover more than any other holiday. Perhaps because it came at the heels of the Persian New Year and somehow felt part of the same festivity. Or perhaps because the family drama made the holiday feel like a theatrical production. At the Seder, like actors, we recited words that conjured no immediate bitter memories to the minds of anyone, save the few elders. This was the 1970s. "Bondage," "affliction," and "suffering at the hands of a bad majority" meant little to most of my family. We vowed "Next year in Israel" but knew, even as the words rang in the air, how hollow they were. The family dreamed of the land of milk and honey but wished to wake up in Tehran. Business was booming, and my uncles, the entrepreneurs, did not want to be fettered by a history that seemed distant now. For nearly half a century, the one hundred thousand Jews of Iran had been sending a representative of their choice to the Majles, the Iranian parliament. They were, at long last, living in any neighborhood they chose, and the one remaining ghetto was far in the south of the city, a place where the poor of every race and creed had settled. Even *najes,* "unclean," the derogatory term by which Muslims had referred to Jews for centuries, was seldom heard in public anymore. Iran was at its most welcoming to Jews in its entire history.

So why even speak of leaving when Tehran's allure was greater than ever? The median income had doubled over the past decade. Largesse was very much in vogue. My Uncle Ardi, the most debonair among the relatives, vied for the check at restaurants, and though he was not alone in trying to grab it, he was often the one to reach into his wallet and quietly pay. Nightlife was flourishing, and between tending to clients by day and romancing women by night, he was also the official family gourmet and walking Zagat. The hosts of the upper Pahlavi Avenue restaurants wasted no time in clearing their best tables for him. At Uncle Ardi's table at the Chattanooga, only those accompanying him were handed menus, because "Beef stroganoff, easy on the cream, followed by the chocolate soufflé" was an order the waiter did not need to hear. When he did not feel like driving, Uncle Ardi walked to the shops across from the University of Tehran. At Arezoumanian's, "the family that unlocked the secret to a good sandwich," his favorite mortadella sandwich was served on a round tray next to a shot of chilled vodka. And before he headed for the office, he stopped not for the traditional tea, yogurt, or sour cherry drink but for a cup of café au lait or something befitting his own ebullient nature, preferably a bottle of Pepsi. By nightfall, long after the secretary had gone home, the tune of the two telephones on his desk switched from daytime duets to solo serenades on his private line. Late into the evening, Uncle Ardi never stopped selling insurance. But what he insured after hours was happiness: a commodity he peddled exclusively at one of several cabarets—on Thursday nights only at Moulin Rouge.

Uncle Ardi was the assimilated Jew. He did not think ghetto

thoughts. He had made a safe passage to the other side and shed the ghetto jobs: he wasn't a butcher or a salesman, a teacher or gold trader—he was an insurance man. He was so assimilated, so certain of his prospects in Iran, that he even insured Muslims. And his rates were some of the most reasonable in town: liability for any four-cylinder vehicle just 500 tomans a year, roughly $80. Six-cylinders: 850 tomans! Guaranteed by Asia Insurance Co., a division of the world-trusted Lloyd's of London.

What Uncle Ardi had really shed was fear; the fear of claiming his share of the good life like any other middle-class citizen. But he did not call it fear. Instead he insisted, "I know how to live." And the place where he knew best how to live, the place he belonged, was Iran. Everything about him was Iranian, to begin with his name: Ardi, short for Ardeshir, the king of an ancient Persian empire. He was so settled that he dared to invest in vanity and buy depreciating goods, like a BMW. No other car would have matched his optimism, the exuberant claim he laid to Tehran. Tehran and no other city. And never more confidently than in 1976.

Naturally, it caused a hilarious uproar at every Seder when Father asked Uncle Ardi to read the Ha Lachma. Everyone burst into laughter long before he began. He obeyed and read, but not without a touch of subversion, a hint of mischief: "This is the bread of affliction—*Some affliction!*—that our forefathers ate in the land of Egypt. This year we are slaves. *May this slavery never end!* This year here and next year at home in Israel. *Pardon me for not packing!*"

Tissues passed from hand to hand as the guests wiped their eyes and roared with laughter. Without missing a beat, Father corrected Uncle Ardi's every word. He was the unruly child Father loved well enough to punish. One man pressed. The other resisted. Neither relented.

What was it, then, that drove us out of Iran? Was it the swastika that appeared on the wall across from our door on the eve of the

1979 revolution? It terrified us, to be sure. But no acts followed the portentous presence on that wall—no rise in hostility among our neighbors or friends. If it was meant to galvanize some latent anti-Semitic feeling among our locals, it failed to do so. Similarly, in 1984, that perfectly Orwellian year, an order came for the washroom facilities in schools to be separated by religion. One morning, as my class filed through the schoolyard, we saw men posting signs above the toilets: Muslims Only. Above the last two stalls, another sign read: Non-Muslims Only. Like the swastika, the signs worried us at first. But they, too, failed to be anything more than a couple of ugly signs. There was an unspoken code among us teenage girls that made abiding by those signs an "uncool" thing to do. Everyone ignored them. With the war against Iraq in its fourth year, the Red Alert sirens shrieking through the school corridors on most days, the school officials, had they even wished, were too busy to enforce washroom rules.

So why did we leave? Not for the reasons our ancestors left biblical Egypt. Nor did we leave for the reasons Jews left modern-day Iraq or Syria—severe persecution subsequent to the establishment of the state of Israel. We left Iran primarily because life under the new circumstances—war and a fundamentalist regime —was becoming gradually intolerable. We left for all the reasons that compelled anyone, whether Gentile or Jew, to leave. Academic and professional opportunities were dwindling for those who did not subscribe to the new ruling ideology, and all the more so for women and members of religious minorities. Though there were no pogroms or overt persecution of Jews in the postrevolutionary era, life for the average non-Muslim proved increasingly stifling and restrictive under the Islamic regime. Yet except for the members of the Baha'i faith, who were blatantly victimized, conditions of living remained bearable.

This is why Iran is still home to the largest community of Jews outside Israel in all of the Middle East. Jews arrived in Iran long before Islam came to exist. And at the dawn of the twenty-first century, nearly twenty thousand Jews continue to live in the country. Along with Christians and Zoroastrians, Jews are considered "people of the Book" and are a legitimate religious minority. To this day, the community sends its own representative to the Majles (whatever a representative may be worth in a land where one man, the supreme leader, has the power to overrule any law or institution). There are synagogues and kosher butcher shops, even several Jewish schools throughout Tehran. However, they are run by Muslim staff and must be kept open on Saturdays.

Like every year since we left Iran, my family will sit at all future Seders here in America. Someone will make a bitter allusion to the past: *Thank God we left unscathed!* Everyone around the table will hasten to agree. All these words will be spoken in Persian. Then the lavish holiday dinner will be served— bowls of eggplant or parsley stew, colorful trays of saffron, cumin, and berry rice. And as the music of Hedieh, Iran's favorite diva, fills the air, they will feverishly compete to tell their stories of the old days.

WOMEN WITHOUT MEN
A Conversation with Shirin Neshat

Shirin Neshat began stirring controversy with her photo se-ries *Women of Allah* (1993-1997). The series drew international attention as well as widespread criticism that Neshat was roman-ticizing Islamic fundamentalism. Neshat moved on to video in-stallations showcasing allegorical narratives about gender issues in Islam. Her work has been exhibited around the world, and she is the recipient of many awards, including the First International Prize at the Venice Biennale in 1999.

You are arguably the most famous Iranian visual artist in the world today. When did you actually leave Iran?
I first left Iran in 1975 to attend high school and then the Uni-versity of California at Berkeley. In the beginning, I went back frequently, until the revolution took place. Then there was a gap of eleven years, from 1979 to 1990, and from that point on, I went every other year. But I haven't been back since 1996.

Why is that?
Doubts about security, about going in and out because of my work.

Have you come under attack by officials in Iran because of your work?
I can't say that I have come under attack, precisely, but it's a del-icate situation. My work was twice exhibited at the Museum of

Contemporary Art in Tehran, and I never suffered any backlash. But then, at other times, I've been warned that my work is too controversial, and that I had better stay away.

In what way is your work controversial?

Mostly because it does not offer one-sided answers, because it challenges our political, and aesthetic, stereotypes. People kept wondering, Iranians especially: What is her position? Is she for or against the revolution? But, purposefully, I was not giving my point of view, and that disturbed many viewers. Take, for example, the series titled *Women of Allah*—photographs I'd shot between 1993 and 1997. These photographs showed veiled women holding guns, with prorevolutionary text inscribed on their bodies. These works were about my perception and understanding of the concept of martyrdom. They were neither pro- nor counterrevolutionary propaganda. They were a visual exploration of what it means ideologically, philosophically, and even aesthetically to be a Muslim woman, a militant, and a martyr. Especially considering that many of these women were doing it voluntarily...

What initially drew you to the subject?

I was mainly interested in the way violence can intersect with religion and spirituality, in the way devotion and the love of God cross paths with cruelty and crime and death. This obsession with death, for me, was an incredible cultural phenomenon. And I wasn't trying to "orientalize" the subject of the Muslim woman or "exoticize" women who are militants—although I was accused, of course, of "romanticizing violence." A lot of Iranians felt that I was making this work because it was very sensational for Western viewers and I wanted to cash in on that. But in reality, I had no career at the time, so I never had an agenda to create this body of work that was going to draw the world's attention. I had no plan to show it; I was doing it for myself.

Why did you choose Iran as the topic—or the context—for your art?

My return to Iran in 1990 changed my life. All these years, I had suffered from a great sense of loss and disconnection with Iran and with my family, and then when I went back, the country had been transformed completely. And I was really frightened by this new country I discovered. Yet for some reason, within this anguish, I found a great purpose. I found that there were many things about it that really drew me and charged me, intellectually and emotionally, and this finally lent me the impulse to make art again. I realized that the reason I wasn't making art anymore was because I felt it was without a purpose; I had nothing to say, nothing to contribute.

What exactly triggered this change?

What was going on in Iran: the turmoil, the energy, the angst. People had endured extremely difficult times, including my family—not only because of the revolution but also because of the Iran-Iraq war. And I was mesmerized by their endurance, the women's especially; so I started reading women writers, traveling through the country, speaking with people, observing their reactions, their gestures, and slowly, I was able to invent my own visual vocabulary, one that would enable me, someday, to express what I saw in my own terms.

Did you feel that something had gone amiss about the image of Iran abroad, and that your images—your films, your photographs—might offer a more subtle focus to the world outside?

I realized how profound this gap was between Iran and its perception abroad. But at the time, I could never have imagined that I would one day have a voice to express the acuteness of this gap, or even address these misrepresentations.

What are some of the most salient misrepresentations that have disturbed you over the years?

Westerners have this sense that Iranian women are submissive victims. But they're not victims, and they're certainly not submissive. In fact, feminism functions in Iran within very different parameters than in Western countries. Iranian women don't compete with men—they don't try to replace men. And while they're fighting hard against oppression, they often get their way, they produce their own solutions. Now, somehow, this whole idea got me into trouble; I would be in places where I'd show my work, and Iranian women in the West would come and see it, and they'd get up and say, "How dare you say that Iranian women are not victims?" What I am saying is this: through their resistance and strength, Iranian women have had a voice in Iranian society, and they continue to have a voice, perhaps more so today than ever before.

It's certainly an interesting phenomenon, and possibly a corollary, that nearly every single well-known Iranian outside of Iran, today, is a woman.
Perhaps those who are more oppressed tend to be more creative about speaking out. And evidently, it's far *harder* for a woman to find a voice in Iran; as writers, artists, or filmmakers, they have to endure far more, in every aspect of life, and therefore their point of view is often more poignant. The men have it easier. And because women are under so much pressure, they end up being more innovative about dealing with crises and devising ways out. They become more subversive, in my mind. For example, in my 1998 black-and-white film *Turbulent,* when the woman sings, she knows she is not allowed to sing like the man, so she finds her own way and sings without an audience, and as a result, she performs music that is completely original and unorthodox.

In 1999, you made *Rapture,* which explores the masculine/feminine paradigm and ends on this lyrical image of women in a desert, pushing a boat to the sea, and leaving the men's citadel behind, for freedom, or perhaps death . . . Then, in 2000, you shot *Fervor,* which was exhibited at the Whitney Museum of American Art's biennial.
Yes, with *Fervor,* I wanted to do one last piece about the question of gender. *Fervor* in particular touched on the question of sexuality and the problematics of temptation in Islamic societies—

Fervor, 2000

Iran especially—where you are constantly required to repress any expression of desire. So I made this film, which brought together two protagonists: a man and a woman. They first see each other in a desert landscape and there is this friction, but they control it, and they each go their own way. Yet oddly, they come across one other again, in a completely distinct situation, at a massive Friday prayer in which men and women are separated, often by a curtain, while a mullah is addressing the audience. Ironically, this man and woman, while seated on each side of a diaphanous curtain, are able to see one another. And again, they feel a friction . . . But as they are going through this very subtle and unspoken flirtation, they find themselves confronted by the preacher, who is telling the story of Joseph and Zalikha; and I picked this story from the Koran, because in it, Zalikha is the one who seduces Joseph, and ultimately, she is blamed for her seduction and his falling into sin. In the film, the preacher uses the story to warn the audience never to be tempted by Satan . . . and yet, just as he is admonishing, this bashful, and deeply erotic, exchange of glances unravels.

After *Fervor,* you moved away from gender issues to delve into more allegorical notions, as in *Tooba,* which was shown at the Asia Society in 2003–2004. What was the inspiration behind *Tooba*?

Just prior to September 11, I had become rather obsessed with the subject of paradise. I had already been thinking a lot about making a film about a garden. My father had a beautiful farm in Iran—a small farm—and I grew up in a garden. Eventually, when my father died, this garden was taken away from my family, and it started to die. It was reduced from an oasis to a half-living, unproductive farm. So I had always had a dream of traveling back to Iran to make a film in that very place. But September 11 happened, and I think I lost all of my romanticism about going back to Iran. Yet this idea of the garden, and the notion of paradise, had infiltrated my mind. And right around September 11, I was asked by an international program to create a work, and I think they really expected me to create a film that dealt directly with the whole complex subject of Islam versus the West coming to a climax. On the contrary, I felt like making a very lyrical piece that somehow, in my mind, still addressed these topics but on a philosophical level. This is how I became interested in the contemporary female novelist Shahrnush Parsipur, who often uses the image of a Tooba in her books, notably in *Tooba and the Meaning of Night.* Then I found out that Tooba is a myth from the Koran. It actually is called the Tree of Paradise; it's a sacred tree, and in Iranian culture it's also a feminine myth, a woman-tree. So I felt that this garden I was trying to construct should also have a Tooba tree in the middle of it, because that was the one tree that would truly make it a paradise. And Islamic and Persian traditions have been crucial in elaborating the idea of gardens as places of transcendence. Consequently, my film *Tooba* gathered three major elements: a sacred garden with a Tooba tree standing on top of a mountain, a large group of men and women who are frenziedly coming toward it from all directions—it's not clear whether they're invading it or seeking refuge—and last, a circle of men already in the garden, who seem like they are people of authority and power and who are dressed in costumes that may be Islamic or Jewish. There is a purposeful lack of clarity: Who are these people? Are they religious? Are they people of politics? Why are they standing inside the garden? Then, somehow, as soon as the mass of people walking toward the garden come into contact with a wall around it, the spirit of the Tooba tree vanishes, and the magic lifts. For me, this piece was about many things. It was about the search for paradise, for a sanctuary, a place of exile, a place of refuge, a community, or a whole world. It was about feeling afraid and vulnerable. And all those people running, in a certain way, represented these feelings. And the characters in the circle are the ones, perhaps, who control our lives, whether in the name of religion or government . . .

And why did you use a two-video installation?
That was more of a conceptual visual device, as I wanted to first separate and isolate the garden and the Tooba tree and then show these forces coming at it. But progressively, as they come closer and closer, the two actually become one, and we understand that it is all happening in the same place. It is not exactly the same image on both screens, but now we understand the geography— "here" and "there" fold together in our minds toward one spatial dimension.

Tooba, 2002

What do you make of the criticism that your art is "reductive" in terms of the ways in which it depicts Iran or Islamic society and philosophy at large?
I've never claimed to have a handle on the meaning of Islam, or the whole complexity of Islam in relation to this world, or even the situation in Iran. I think it's more about me understanding my status and having something personal invested in my work. I feel like much of this work is intimate and deeply existential in that sense. So I don't feel a responsibility to be an advocate or an ambassador in any way. And I believe that my work has to be considered from the binary position of the artist and the exile, simply because my point of view is contingent on this binary position. For example, I will never be able to convey a completely "accurate" reflection or information about Iran, since I don't live there; I live far away. Thus my perspective and my fiction are colored by all kinds of influences, of personal experiences I've had. But no matter, I feel that as an Iranian, I'm entitled to address

subjects that are about my country. And obviously, for someone who doesn't have access to home, home becomes a great obsession. Besides, Iranian politics have radically defined and shaped my life. So regardless of where I live, I am a part of Iran, and I am engaged with the future of my country, and I have something to say. But what I have to say is very much within the parameter of who I am, and what my life has been on the outside—and that's my voice.

Is your work as an artist to personalize and even blur the "messages" as much as possible? Is that the best way of deconstructing and dispelling clichés about Iran?
Absolutely. Just when the viewer's preconception is that Iranian women are victims, for instance, you put the armor on these women and thwart the preconception. This is how I've moved forward.

And now you're working on your first feature film?
Yes, it's based on a book called *Women Without Men,* written by Shahrnush Parsipur in the early 1990s. It's a story about the lives of five women from distinct social backgrounds who all have had complex and difficult pasts. The story takes place in 1953. One of the women dreams of being famous, although she has no talent and is reaching menopause; another is frightened of sex and men and romantic love, and she eventually decides to become a tree, since a tree can have seeds and bear fruit without suffering intercourse; then there is the prostitute who's been a prostitute ever since childhood, and she's living in a brothel and carries so much guilt about who she is that one day she sees one of her clients as faceless and headless, and she thinks God is punishing her; there is also a religious woman who is controlled and repressed by her conservative family; and finally, there is another middle-class religious woman whose obsession is simply to marry the man she loves. So one way or another, these women end up running away from their lives. And mysteriously, there is

one man, a gardener, who becomes involved in bringing these women together in a mystic garden in the region of Karaj. Each woman arrives at the garden burdened with her unspoken dreams and nightmares. And together, they strive to create their own world, their own utopia, with their own rules. Thus the garden becomes a sanctuary, a place of exile, a place of time-out for these women to recollect and reassert themselves before once again resuming the paths of their "real" lives . . .

This book was banned in Iran?
Yes, and Shahrnush has been to prison a few times because of this book. She is now living in exile.

The story is a beautiful parable, and it's narratively intricate. Why did you choose to make a feature film instead of your previous art films?
As an artist, I'm quite restless. I don't usually do anything for very long. For example, when I was doing photography, just as it became known, I turned my back on it and started making video. Now that I've made several video installations that are all dealing with multiple screens, I need to challenge myself again, and I'm very interested in this possible fusion of cinema and visual arts. The idea is to carve my own visual style in this format. But I also feel that this is an important book that has not been widely read. And I want to breathe some life into it and present it to the public's gaze. It's political, it's very philosophical, it's spiritual, it's mystical. And more than anything, it's extraordinarily universal. It's a universal tale, and it's possible for me, at this point, to bring in elements from my own culture and lend them a meaning that transcends the frontiers of Iran.

Are you tired of being typecast as an "Iranian artist"?
Being Iranian is not the be-all and end-all of my work. And I think, for all of us who work in art, as much as we want to stay true and responsible to our cultures and explain our work at times

through the cultural lens, ultimately, the staying power of the works will be determined and perpetuated above and beyond our national boundaries.

The philosopher Theodor Adorno wrote that the only way to reach the universal in aesthetics is to dwell on the particular...

Yes, I think that is the greatest challenge for an artist, because you first need to run the gamut of unfamiliarity—but then, within that unfamiliarity, you need to somehow open a luminous little passage and conjure up an ancient sense of recognition and familiarity, which we may unabashedly call "universality."

SEX IN THE TIME
OF MULLAHS

Azadeh Moaveni

"You came for the politics, but you will stay for the nightlife," my friend Davar informed me one sultry summer evening in Tehran, shortly after my return to Iran. Sooner or later, if you are an Iranian living outside, someone will inform you of all that you have been missing in the Islamic Republic: a sexual revolution behind closed doors, where young Iranians drop ecstasy, host backroom orgies, and generally put Amsterdam to shame. If you raise your eyebrows, as I did with Davar, you will then be presented with stories of how diverse the party scene in Iran is— not just confined to Tehran but encompassing ski resorts and the Caspian waterfront (vodka!...caviar!...opium!...beneath it all, can't you see how much *fun* we're having?) Typically, it is a worrisome sign when people are not content to merely experience pleasure but must loudly proclaim that they are sloshing around in it "five nights a week at least." I chalked this up to the urge of young Iranians to broadcast their freewheeling lifestyle —an overcompensation for the dreary martyr kitsch that hung across Tehran—and obediently followed Davar into the hazy Tehran night.

It took a good hour and a half to reach our destination, a *bagh* in Karaj, just outside Tehran; baghs, or the expansive, shaded gardens people could afford when they lived in the outer suburbs, are preferred party locales. Because of their distance from the main roads, they are patrolled less frequently by young policemen who revel in the temporary sense of power breaking up parties grants them—watching the ashen women scramble for their veils, men clearing away bottles of homemade booze with nervous fingers. Davar preferred earthy parties with more diverse crowds to the arid, high-end soirées of north Tehran, and he grinned uncharacteristically all the way to the bagh, perked up as he was by the endorphin rush of an afternoon soccer game. He even laughed as we passed a billboard with David Beckham advertising motor fuel, his magic legs draped in black cloth. It had been considered unseemly for Beckham's bare legs to grace urban Tehran, and virtue was returned to the city overnight when all the billboards acquired scarves. Davar was working two jobs to buy off his military service, yearning for the West to ease its visa restrictions so that his brain could also be drained. As a lover of Beckham, as an angry vessel of too many unmet expectations, such sights reminded him of why he could not stand to stay here—in a country run by clerics who sought to erase Beckham's naked knees but could not devote attention to providing him, Davar, with a viable future.

We entered the house, each of us looking for people we knew. The angsty female host was humming along to Dido, but a younger gaggle of girls—all exposed, shimmery limbs—demanded something more lively and familiar, which to them meant "Nastaran," the Persian pop hit of that year whose lyrics, "You don't even know what you really want," seemed to resonate with the general mood. The bagh was divided into a few cliques: an artsy corner, a pounding-down-the-vodka corner, and a rave area where those on happy drugs merrily surrendered the centuries-old Iranian obsession with privacy and clung to each other, as though they had just discovered their flesh was velvet. Davar honed in on his target, a young divorcée he'd met at a previous party and eagerly invited to this one. She had thick wrists and a cartoonlike beauty, as if she had been drawn by a talented child. He enjoyed an hour of small talk, working his way toward possible conquest, toward the consummation of an act that would, however briefly, restore his sense of autonomy, display his total disregard for the regime's taboos, allow him to say to the world, or to himself, "I am not just another twenty-five-year-old Iranian making a $300-a-month salary that I can't get married on, in a country that offers me no joyful or remunerative opportunity."

Exit Davar and the divorcée. She kept looking over her shoulder anxiously, likely wondering whether anyone would notice them disappearing into a back room. Enter a prominent reformist writer known for showing up at parties with women half his age and drinking until his red-rimmed eyes rolled backward in his head. It is fashionable for married reformist intellectuals, even the once-pious revolutionaries, to display girlfriends. This signals no broadening of their attitudes toward women and sexuality, however; on those questions, they are still predictably orthodox. The reformist in the room before us, with his smooth-skinned lover, had once mocked a friend of mine for recommending a Fellini film. "If you want to watch sexy movies, why don't you just say you want to watch sexy movies?" he'd said, chuckling. Reformists like him consider Karl Popper the Truth, Fellini pornography, and any suggestion that politics and sexuality intersect as lust sublimated by political philosophy.

Enter a young, talented painter with working-class south Tehran roots—the only person I'd ever known to be thrown out of a party by the hosts rather than the morality police. In the sordid atmosphere of these turn-of-the-millennium Tehran parties, people behave with such breathtaking shamelessness that it takes a lot to get yourself ejected for misbehaving. The painter, whose female relatives wore the chador and offered no understanding into the erotic rituals of these bare-haired, Dido-listening women of middle Tehran, had assumed these parties were sexual free-for-alls. At a recent gathering, he had guided someone's visiting cousin to a bedroom early in the evening, and at the night's end had beckoned another—a friend of the first woman—with similar horizontal ambitions. The second course, feeling like a second choice, declaimed loudly that he had no shame (an altogether more serious charge in Persian than in English) and had him swiftly removed from the party.

Where was I in all this? On a pile of cushions, observing the silvery reformist with his bookish Lolita, the predatory painter, the wooden door to the room where Davar had disappeared with his divorcée. Observing how at once sullen and alive it all seemed. Alive because people had carved out a space where they could drop their layers of pretense. Sullen because their revelry was tinged with more darkness than light, reflecting all the thwarted ambitions, the lost opportunities, the violations and stolen freedoms that defined their reality outside. There was no sparkly air of carefree fun here. In the pressing of flesh people were negotiating far more than pleasure—they were trying to assert free will, anxious to feel included in something that was not sheerly a grotesque lie.

Eventually, Davar emerged from the recesses of the house, and I presented him with my impression about the evening: "The Islamic Republic has killed romance."

He fixed me with an irritated look that meant "I have brought you to a party and you are whining loftily."

"Seriously," I said, "think about it. The post-1979 generation has grown up without ever seeing a modern Iranian actor kiss on the screen; kissing in public is illegal; being alone with a man or a woman is a premeditated act, driven by logistics rather than passion—securing location, getting there and back unmolested, and in the case of that one over there"—I nodded toward the reformist—"packing Viagra." For a country where recreational sex is discouraged, its accessories—Viagra, birth control pills (sans prescription), opiates of various kinds—are as easy and cheap to come by as cigarettes. The Islamic Republic has killed so much that was vital—intellectuals, legal rights, peace of mind—that the death of romance, or at least of romantic spontaneity, is often overlooked.

On the drive over, I had asked Davar how he knew the divorcée might be open to his advances. "Well, she wasn't so opposed last time," he replied.

"Last time?"

"Yeah, we both ended up staying too late and didn't have much else to do while waiting for sunrise."

Sooner or later, if you socialize after dark in Tehran and consume alcohol, you will need to spend a slice of the night at your host's home. The dark hours between one and five a.m. are more difficult to navigate, as the sober teenagers and families who crawl the city until midnight have gone to bed, and anyone driving home tipsy or high or merely in the company of a nonspouse becomes low-hanging fruit for the police and paramilitaries on the streets. Many erotic escapades trace their origins to being marooned together during these hours at some acquaintance's home; and if there is only one guest remaining, sometimes the gracious host, in the long-standing tradition of Iranian hospitality, feels obliged to invite the odd straggler to bed.

A couple of weeks after that night, Davar let me pick the party. A friend of a friend was hosting a *bal masqué* at his lofted north Tehran apartment, a peculiar party theme, especially since being outside—for which this occasion was meant to be a remedy—was *already* a masquerade. That evening, the look was more Indo-Eurotrash, as the men and women twirling masks floated about theatrically, purring things to each other in multiple languages.

The crowd was more privileged and thus much less concerned with what actually was happening in the country. The only semipolitical comment I heard all evening was from another writer, who told me he had recently met a cleric who'd programmed a special farting ring-tone on his mobile for women callers. At these parties, the women tend to be in their thirties, brows smoothed by Botox, and seeking desperately to conceal their sexual histories. That is because most of them are as yet unmarried and keep secret from even their closest girlfriends (also rivals in the marriage sweepstakes) the truth about whose beds they have or have not shared. "We are leaving tomorrow for the south of France," a woman in a sequined feathered mask announced to the room, in the tone of a socialite who lives to announce this sort of thing, but she'd forgotten she was masked and that therefore people cared even less than usual.

I tried to imagine what such a party would have been like before 1979; it didn't take very long, because my sense was: exactly the same. Today, these are the parties visiting journalists and diaspora-caste Iranians often attend, the people who stand out for their flamboyant contrast to the "I love martyrdom" mural-clad Tehran outside—feathers and masks and cleavage and lines of cocaine, the milieu where the sexual free-for-all or revolution or whatever you choose to call it is supposedly taking place. But it isn't. This is the realm where time has stood still, where north Tehranis observe the defining rule of Iranian culture—reality is taboo—and conduct themselves with urbane calculation. Here privacy is guarded militantly, the practice of disguising oneself in layer upon social layer unchanged.

Iran's actual sexual revolution is to be found in the baghs and low-rise cement apartment blocks where ordinary young people openly swap lovers. By practicing premarital sex into their twenties and beyond, and by not seeking to conceal it (at least among themselves), it is middle-class young Iranians who are pioneering the sexual frontier. In the era of postrevolution economic decline, the average marriage age has jumped, and young men and women face a long stretch of single years their parents were never forced to contend with. In the contest between traditional sexual mores and pheromones, the latter have long since won out, and at any given moment in Tehran, tens of thousands of youths like Davar and his friends share the keys to modest *garçonnières.* Behind those walls, there are no designer labels, no expensive stereos, none of the trappings of the storied hedonism that would have you believe Iran's erotic evolution is cinematic or particularly Western. If anything, it is an indigenous way of coping with the Islamic Republic, of reclaiming the freedoms that have been stifled, of filling the void of opportunities lost. For Davar, my guide to the Tehran nights, it was a way to make up for all other opportunities denied him, all other opportunities being held hostage in the Islamic Republic.

Late on one of the many evenings I declined to accompany him, he called as I was skimming through the poems of Forugh Farrokhzad. In her lines, which I read to him over the scratchy connection, she wrote that when her life had become nothing but the tick-tock of a clock, she discovered she "Must love, Insanely."

MISREADING KUNDERA IN TEHRAN

Naghmeh Zarbafian

Once upon a time in Washington I met Harold, who did not like poetry. At an Indian restaurant he spoke to me of politics, which were of no interest to my mind, yet he went on to comment on my situation in a society I have lived in for twenty years. And I found myself responding to him in a way I would never do to a stranger. My whole life started to pass before my eyes. The personal aspect of politics was what I could not neglect. He brought up a new aspect of what I disliked.

When we started the second course of our meal in that dim restaurant, I read one of my poems to him and tried to unfold some of its hidden layers and meanings. Then I asked him to tell me his own impressions about another poem of mine. He said he was scared, yet he pinpointed some of the most important parts of the poem and made some purely unique observations about it. "You gave me hope," he said as we left the restaurant.

And I had his words with me when at the Tehran airport they took away my passport and held me and some other young boys and girls for three hours, ransacking my luggage and interrogating me thoroughly about all the traces of Western culture I had brought in my suitcase as well as my personal life: the reason why I went to the United States and the books I brought to Iran, the people I met in the United States and the pictures I brought to Iran, the amount of money I spent in the United States and the audiotapes I brought to Iran. My suitcases were rummaged as well as my family background; my books were checked as well as my career. My entire identity was inspected before I was set free, before I, seemingly, was allowed to reclaim my passport, my name, and my individuality. And before I was given back my tapes: tapes now completely erased by the morality police —among them, the Irish songs that Harold had given me as a souvenir.

Listening to Harold's erased tape now, I feel that they have crushed the words we had exchanged. Dissecting the tape, they have dissected the dialogue, a singular moment of mutual understanding and enjoyment that was to be continued in a piece of music. Harold and I had opened two different worlds to one another. Though we belonged to separate spheres, oceans apart, I had his favorite music and he had my poem to keep our dialogue—as well as our memories—alive. We were closely related to one another through some small pieces of art. We, each of us with different backgrounds, different nationalities, different ideas, different cultures, different religions, and different ages, came together in a unique moment. Our inner selves met in spite of all the discrepancies. So it was not just the tape that was destroyed but our relationship; my relationship to "the other." Thus finishes the first episode of my story.

I leave my characters, Harold and the morality police of the airport, to their disparate worlds, thinking of how "the other" —no matter who or what—can be considered the enemy: and music, words, and images the enemy's weapons. Now to confront this enemy, I have no choice but to close the doors, hide in my cell, and choke the enemy's voice. Yet this is not my responsibility. Apart from the morality police, some other people who are superior to us are here to recognize "the enemy" and close our eyes to it. These superior people belong to the Ministry of Islamic Culture and Guidance, without whose official permission no books or magazines are published, no audiotapes are distributed, no movies are shown, and no cultural organization is established. Imagine the place as a castle on a mountaintop, close to heaven, with an aura of sacredness, and chockful of people—all eyes and ears—looking down upon us, deciding what we should read, see, and listen to, what we should enjoy and what we should not. Our guardian angels, here to guide us and protect our culture from the enemy, "the other." Yet as the advocates of a dialogue among civilizations (a phrase coined by our former president, Mohammad Khatami, thanks to whom the year 2001 is now called "the year of dialogue among civilizations"), we should also welcome "the other."

So the door should not be completely locked. And in this ajar relationship, certain strategies should be applied to make the "alien culture" adjustable. But in our daily lives, Western literature—as one of the manifestations of this culture—goes through the selfsame process, executed not only by the superior people of the Ministry of Islamic Culture and Guidance and the morality police but also by the translators, and sometimes even by the readers themselves.

Before examining the way this kind of literature is represented in Iran, I will narrate the second episode of my tale, which opens to a novel by Milan Kundera titled *Identity*. The main characters are a man and a woman, Jean-Marc and Chantal, and the story is about the ups and downs of their relationship. Chantal feels that nobody is attracted to her because she is getting old. And this is painful to her, so she lets Jean-Marc, the man she is in love with, know about her fears. Then comes a series of anonymous love letters for Chantal. Hiding them from Jean-Marc, she tries to discover her unknown correspondent and is mistaken about his identity several times. When she finds out that Jean-Marc has written the letters, she feels that he has violated her privacy. Jean-Marc, on the other hand, feels enraged by her response to another man, the writer of letters, who is, ironically, his own creation. And the whole novel centers on the fact that two people in love, at their most intimate moments, feel that they do not recognize one another's identity, that their voices come from far off, that each moment bears the fright of losing the loved one: Chantal feels nostalgic for Jean-Marc while he is sitting before her eyes, and Jean-Marc sees her as a shadow, a familiar woman with a stranger's face.

On the verge of dream and reality, the characters at last reach a point where they do not know whether or not they have dreamed the story. So in comes the narrator in the final chapters to intensify the ambiguity of the situation by posing several questions to the reader about his dream-real story. The voice of the narrator travels through the minds of the two characters, embodying each of their voices. Each chapter is devoted to one voice and each voice is like a half circle, completed by the other voice in another chapter. Thus are related the thoughts. Thus are related the events. Thus is created the structure of the novel behind which Kundera is smiling, not knowing what happens to the identity of his narrative when unfurled in a country so far removed from his own.

The next episode of my story takes place in the realm of the same novel, yet in a different language. The translation of *Identity* into Persian opens a new world but not merely because of linguistic differences. Opening the door to the translated world of the novel, the same characters with the same names in the same setting emerge, yet the world looks strange. Chapters are deleted, paragraphs are misplaced, and words are mistranslated, forming chasms that can never be filled. As a result, the two books are remote from one another; one is a blurry shadow of the other. A misty atmosphere covers the translated version because of the way words are manipulated.

The translator misuses the language by stripping away its passion and slowing down its rhythm. This is mostly manifested in the relationship of the two lovers, to achieve whose separation each and every trick is used. Chantal's "clasping against Jean-Marc" is turned into a sheer "getting close to him." Jean-Marc's holding Chantal to "his body" is turned into his holding her to "him." If here Jean-Marc "touches her with his lips," there—in the faraway translated world—he just "fondles" her. So the sentences are not re-created in the second language; instead, it seems that each word has withered under the touch of some eerie fingers.

In one of their love scenes, Chantal and Jean-Marc, in a kind of game, chase one another in the apartment. We, in this distant country, are also watching them, but as soon as they go to bed, the game stops in our world. We do not see anything. He does not make love to her in our world but just "declares his affection"; the "act of love" is shorn of all its tension and excitement. The tension of action is thus removed, and what remains is a mere declaration. And, of course, we never hear that she cries out in climax. Instead of this, there is an empty space and then comes the next chapter, in which the sun rises—too early for us. Yet the words "procreate," "copulate," and "coitus," described by one of the characters as "the sole purpose of human life," are not censored. Neither is the word "rape." To the translator and the censor, these words are the harmless ones. So sex as a dialogue between two bodies is cut off, whereas the aspect of sex that deals with banality and violence is "morally" approvable.

The destruction of details does not occur only in the love scenes. The details that conjure up the atmosphere of the lovers' dialogue are also missing. What they drink and toast to is a mystery to the safe corner of our world. Each type of drink, whether champagne, enhancing the joyous excitement of Chantal and Jean-Marc's first encounter; or cognac, darkening a gloomy sentiment when they speak of death; or wine, as a background to their light conversation, is just a "drink," unspecified. A life with no nuances is manifested in the deletion of these concrete, minute details.

Nuances of feelings suffer from the same lack. Chantal has ambiguous feelings for Jean-Marc in the novel. With him "life weighs on her," and without him she will be "condemned to live." Yet neither the fictional characters nor the others—the readers—have the right, in our world, to demean life or bear it as a burden. Hence no traces of such emotions can be found in the translated novel.

The one-sidedness of things in the translated version makes for a sort of ideological absolutism. In its original form, this absolutism manifests itself sometimes in an immutability of feelings and sometimes in an everlasting sacredness of concepts. In one of his love letters, Jean-Marc pictures Chantal covered in a cardinal's red mantle. His "gorgeous cardinal," he calls her. In his letter in the translated world, however, he never writes this but rather mentions that red is his favorite color: the beautiful color of cardinals, he adds. So the female character is entirely eliminated in the elongated version of that three-word phrase expressing Jean-Marc's love for Chantal, a love that surpasses religion or, in a way, becomes his religion. Elsewhere in the novel, Chantal pictures herself as a "lecherous cardinal." Again, the translator prefers to picture her the other way around: "a sinful creature wearing the cardinal's mantle." The word "cardinal" is associated with religion. Thus, once translated, its sacredness is preserved through all kinds of ridiculous manipulations.

The representation of an orgy in such a mute world is yet another story. The word "orgy" itself is vaguely translated as "party." In the final chapters of the original novel, Chantal is trapped in a house where an orgy is under way. Terrified and naked, she is running through the labyrinthine structure of the house trying to find a way out. Naked among strangers, she has no idea where she is and what her name is, like a baby born to a bizarre world, searching for the voice of a man—whom she does not remember either—to call her name, to give her back her identity.

In the translated version, however, Chantal's nakedness as well as the others'– the main characteristic of such a gathering—is entirely omitted. Consequently her running in the corridors of an outlandish house in search of a way out is quite meaningless to the reader, who has no idea about the orgy. Avoiding any mention of her nakedness makes the scene frightening, but not in the way the author intended. Chantal's naked encounter with an odd multitude of people in a nightmarish world causes her horror, the very horror that results in her loss of identity. The translated version also conveys horror, yet it is a different horror. The reader hardly knows where she is, what she is escaping from, and why she is terrified. The loss of identity, here, occurs in the minds of the readers themselves: they, too, are trapped in an unknown world where they cannot figure out whom they are facing, what is happening, and how it is happening. And instead of the novel, a misty face is before them, with which they can hardly entertain a dialogue.

There is no writer before the reader; in his place, there are several puppeteers, playing with the writer and his characters, putting words in their mouths and thoughts in their mind, or wiping them away. The puppeteers not only move the characters when they should not and still them when they should not, they also disregard the writer himself, shattering the world he has created.

Kundera's readers in Tehran make their way into the last episode of my story, which leaves the fictional domain; here comes, allegedly, the real one. Setting: Tehran, February 2000. From the blurry atmosphere of the translated novel we step into a faintly lit room, containing stern faces, unfamiliar to one another, yet all of them seemingly familiar with Kundera's novels in translation. They are the characters of this episode: some brilliant students of art and literature in their twenties and thirties.

How does Kundera's voice feel to them? This is the question launching the discussion, opening the doors to a dialogue. From the dialogue between the characters to a dialogue among us, the younger generation of a country thousands of miles away from Kundera's, sitting in this dusky room on a winter night. They have all enjoyed reading the translated novel, not knowing that it was fabricated. The discussion starts with the question of human relations.

Some of these readers try to remain aloof, either by not talking about the relationship of Chantal and Jean-Marc or by talking about it objectively, generalizing and philosophizing over it. Hiding behind abstract words or bombastic quotations, they avoid expressing their own selves in relation to love. Yet two of them—Kaveh, a young publisher, and Ali, a grad student of English literature—speak about their personal experiences. Both of them had fallen in love with two girls and had lost them. The fact that two of these young men, in discussing the novel, are reminded of their unfulfilled relationships is interesting. Their incomplete encounter with a love story in a novel corresponds to their personal experiences.

The translated Chantal and Jean-Marc also evoke other responses, different on the surface yet tinted with the same implications: "Their love is heavenly and sacred. Nothing is new about their relationship. It is exactly like in our classical literature. Only the form has changed, that is, an earthly shape is lent to an ethereal concept," says Ahmad, a young architect. "These two characters are two sides of the same thing, united and fused together as one," he adds. Ramin, a student of architecture, believes: "This story is harmonious with our feelings and our time, showing us something that we knew before, yet did not know how to express. The characters act the way we do. That's why I like it. In this novel, I find my own values as a contemporary man." According to Ziba, another student of architecture, who finds the characters "very interesting because they are down-to-earth," such relationships (living together without being married) do not exist in Iran. But it makes no difference. The characters look like a married couple.

They have all identified with these characters, which are not the "real" characters of Kundera's fictional world. They have even identified what they take to be Kundera's characters with those of classical Iranian literature: "the same as our life, the same as us, the same as our literature." Searching for this sameness while encountering the other is the common theme in their views on the novel. The safe corner of this sameness has protected most of them from facing a different world. And this sameness is partially constructed by the cooperation of the translator and the censor. The rest is the curtain covering the readers' eyes, a cover that rejects the far away and the unfamiliar, a cover that veils the differences, obscuring them in such a manner that they may look familiar. A cover that once seemed artificial and imposed by the outside world—the world of the ruling system—has now become an interior cover.

It is not just at the airport that one is stripped of any sounds, images, or words that are tinged with "the other"—one is even stripped of some most intimate moments in a private room during the personal experience of reading a novel. The inability to break free of their own reality prevents readers from facing Chantal and Jean-Marc as they are—two European characters of the late twentieth century—and causes them to envelop these characters in the recognizable features of classical Persian love stories of centuries ago. It also causes them to misread such an earthly love as heavenly, to disregard the gaps inserted by the translator/censor in the twists and turns of the lovers' dialogue, and finally, to dismiss the necessity of having personal privacy for the continuation of this dialogue.

In the novel, the two characters suffer from this lack of privacy. Outside the novel, few readers consider this lack. Unconsciously, they are pointing to something they themselves lack, since they are the victims of the disruption of privacy as readers of a novel whose very privacy is excised. Soha, a grad student of English literature, states: "When I go out, carrying my journal, a newspaper, or a book, I am constantly on guard, thinking that sooner or later somebody will arrest and interrogate me about them." When the personal domains of each individual are constantly stripped, self-expression, too, becomes nearly impossible. Nina, another student of architecture and the most silent participant of this gathering, is fascinated by the way the characters express their inner selves and enter "the forbidden territories." She feels the need to open up the most hidden parts of her own self. In her tone there is an undercurrent—a longing for excitement, for "walking on a thin rope." Ziba admires the characters' daring self-expression. "I usually censor myself." Most however, do not say a word about it, being used to unprivate lives, lives whose every detail is monitored: from the color of the clothes they wear to the identity of the person they laugh with on the street to the music they listen to in their cars and the movies they watch on their VCRs. Their private spheres are shaken and shattered by constant interference. But how can they carry on a dialogue without nurturing first a genuine, unspoiled self? How can they communicate with a text when they do not face it in its entirety? And how can they discover the gaps in the text? The gaps that correspond to the gaps in their inner selves. So is justified their unconcern for the form of the novel.

To these readers of Kundera's *Identity,* content is the most prominent aspect of the novel, to the extent that they consider the form unimportant. Some point out the novel's lack of structure, some call it puzzling, and some do not mention it at all. The aesthetic pleasure of the novel diminishes behind their abstract discussions. Surely, to those hands that cut away or manipulate pieces of the novel, delete chapters or combine irrelevant paragraphs, no such thing as aesthetic structure exists. The book itself is presented as formless. And the responses of these readers, too, are as fragmented and shapeless as the text they are faced with. No wonder that the novel's form seems the least important aspect in their eyes. No wonder that they do not suspect the existence of gaps or else simply take them for granted.

No one talks of the book as an incomplete entity. No one refers to the strangeness of the characters' relationship. No one even mentions the incomprehensibility of the damaged parts. Instead, they justify the vagueness of all those chapters as the "complexity" of the novel or the indispensable elusiveness created by the writer himself. They, as readers, think that they should fill the gaps themselves.

So I enter the dialogue as another character. I, too, have been trapped in this fake world. I, too, have enjoyed it. And my enjoyment was such that I decided to acquire the original version of the novel and read it over and over again, although this enjoyment in turn was totally shattered. And out of the scattered pieces of that enjoyment this story emerged. The story in which I, too, play a role. On a dark winter night, I enter the dialogue to tell them of my own experience with the novel, unraveling the whole story, including the omitted parts and the manipulated ones. The real fictional world of the novel is disclosed. But except for Bahar, another student of architecture, who has done a detailed study of the novel and is now deeply shocked, the rest remain indifferent.

"Knowing these parts won't open a new door to me and it won't shed new light upon the novel," says Ramin, who strongly believes that he can fill the gaps himself. Ahmad, who prefers to talk about every school of philosophy rather than his own self and his own impressions, reluctantly states: "Even if I had read those parts, the book wouldn't have changed for me. The only important point about these parts is their didactic aspect. Reading them, we learn what we should not do." To Soha, the censored parts are very "loathsome." "I prefer to read the translated version the way it is, otherwise I'm not quite sure if I can like it," she adds and hastily changes the subject. Ziba doesn't care for the explicitness of these parts. She finds them very "earthly." "I've heard that this is morally the purest novel by Kundera. It is devoid of any immoral points and if there are any, they won't go beyond the verbal domain," she says.

Kaveh puts an end to the entire discussion when he derisively blurts: "This is the way we have read novels for years. And this is the way it will be. Why fuss so much over it?" Silence. Silence. Silence.

On one side of the dialogue is a voice in search of another. Sometimes this searching voice—in this case, the voice of the reader—is satisfied with what he or she hears, or has no choice but to feel satisfied. And this satisfaction is aroused not by the encounter with another voice but, to some extent, by the echo of his or her own, mistaken for that of "the other." So the dialogue that was to shape an identity, to illuminate a sense of self-awareness through an encounter with the other turns into a monologue shaped by the translator and the censor. They are the ones, in the end, who are faced with "the other" in its real, unfamiliar guise, prior to the reader and superior for having the right to reshape "the other's" world. This distorted world is then presented to the reader in such a form that any traces of the original work may seem disturbing, unnecessary, or less appealing. Through this miscommunication, the other side remains aloof, on the far side of the boundary, where it stood well before being masqueraded on our side, in Iran.

Of that entity—"the other"—only some bits and pieces are taken, an effigy of a live being. On this side of the boundary, there is another live being, a reader, who expects to encounter the totality of an unfamiliar being when faced with it. Readers cannot find it, nor could they communicate with it if they did. And both remain lonely creatures on two sides of a bridge that is hardly built. There is just an illusion of dialogue, with voices that remain misheard or unheard. A reader who communicates with fragments of wreckage called a translated novel.

In the final chapter of Kundera's *Identity,* the narrator ends the story in an uncertain atmosphere, meandering between dream and reality. "Whose dream was this story?" he asks. I have no answer, looking at myself and the remaining characters—we have all been trapped among the pages of a book we never wanted to be a part of. Whose dream are we? Do we belong to that dream? Are we possessed by it? Or is there a dream belonging to each and every one of us?

I have a vision. It looks like a flickering light. It looks like the vanishing dew you can never touch, no matter how close you get. And I would like to finish my story with an untold number of shapes I can see in this little drop of dew I found once upon a time.

The next chapter of my story will be a fairy tale.

RECEDING WORLDS

Daryush Shayegan

The following letters are taken from Daryush Shayegan's autobiographical narrative, *Land of Mirages*. Through a correspondence between two lovers who have parted because of insidious cultural rifts, Shayegan offers a portrait of contemporary Iran. Kaveh is Iranian and lives in Tehran; Marianne, who is French, has returned to her home country after a long stay in Iran that proved beguiling at first, then all but intolerable. Kaveh is now torn between his tenderness for Marianne and the dim promise of a relationship with Afsaneh. But above all, he is gnawed by melancholia and a sense of resignation at the prospect of his own millennial yet regressive culture.

Paris, February 26, 1997

My darling Kaveh,

I received your letter dated February 23 on the very next day. No doubt a passenger from Tehran placed it in my box without introducing himself. I rush to respond straight away, but let me first ask you this: why do we need to cross paths without understanding one another? Are our respective worlds so incommensurable? Are we not inhabitants of the same lands, do we not even speak the same language? You perfectly master ours, and one might almost mistake you for a Frenchman, although you drag behind you a nimbus of misunderstandings. When you found yourself in my homeland, I saw you undertake a few performances here and there, with firmness and a certain brio. And yet, you always remained absent.

You obstinately refused to take part in collective life; the problems of the public sphere were surely of interest to you, but only from a distance. Your engagement had a provisional gleam, as though you were willing to lend yourself while never actually giving yourself. You witnessed everything through the amplifying prism of comparison. Almost perversely, you accentuated differences that were often insignificant in my eyes, whereas in yours they took on primordial importance. If someone made a disagreeable remark on a particular topic or behaved in an inelegant manner to your mind, if someone lacked availability for a particular meeting or remained indifferent to the solicitude of "the other," you promptly got on your high horse: you immediately opposed your "humanity" to ours. You used to say: Europeans exchange ideas as though they are standing in some marketplace, but they know nothing of true friendship, which is a communion between beings. Europeans are intelligent, at times too intelligent, but they lack wisdom; they are tolerant but they do not know compassion; they are honest but they are not "lords." I can enumerate a thousand other biting remarks, at times terribly right, which you emitted with regard to us. They irritated me, amused me, offended me, and often gave me food for thought! I told myself you certainly had reasons of your own. I tried to understand the meaning of your criticism; I applied myself to the task and finally gathered that what you reproached us with was not related to individuals so much as to the type of civilization to which we belong. I realized that the same defects that you vehemently denounced and against which you revolted emanated precisely from the depersonalized rule of law that we have constructed throughout the centuries: that these very "lacunas" were the salutary barriers behind which you had come to seek protection when you found yourself at the mercy of the most radical form of arbitrary governance. Here, my dear Kaveh, lies the great paradox of your life: you had fled what you loved to find refuge in a haven you defied at times in quite a cavalier fashion.

And yet, dear Kaveh, your discourse, just like your shifting temperament, was never one-dimensional. Sometimes you went into back gear, you directed your thunders against your own compatriots. "To be an autonomous subject, *that* is the great affair," you said, "rather than wallow in the swamps of our own insane atavisms!" So I wondered if these two worlds did not, in fact, develop to the detriment of one another; and after all, you knew close to nothing about it. When I came to live in Iran, in your country, I soon grasped the inevitable irony: the usefulness of one model and the simultaneous fascination for the other. I also became conscious that, for the moment, their coexistence was nearly impossible. That one cannot be a citizen without being a bourgeois and that, to be a lord, one needs to possess slaves.

At present, dear friend, we entertain the same wounds; only our harbors are distinct. You have found your tribe and you keep cursing it for its gregarious instinct. As for me, I have found my civil security and I languish for the land of chimeras . . .

Farewell, my handsome friend.

Tehran, March 27, 1959

My dearest Marianne,

The year 1378 of the solar Hegira has just drawn to a close. At times it seems to me that we live, mentally, in the fourteenth century of the Christian era or even a century prior to the great upheaval of the Italian quattrocento.

The days go by with such extraordinary monotony that my head wavers every so often. I wonder if we could stop the incessant flow of this process—which, in reality, is not a process since it does nothing but repeat itself with painstaking stubbornness. Apart from the rare and brief moments of happiness that I am granted by the beloved presence of one person or another or by some captivating book, the rest of the hours are numbingly sterile. To which I should add the mediocrity of the political situation, which, in spite of the president's dull speeches, remains superbly stilted. People say that what he performs is logotherapy, that mores are evolving indeed—pressure is dwindling on women, they wear the occasional makeup and feel free to flaunt brighter colors —but nothing actually changes. No sooner have you taken a few steps forward than you immediately have to turn back on your heels as though you had trespassed over some threshold; for any step forward is a possible threat to the natural inertia of things—stagnation, pure and simple. Yet I know that in the slits of this apparent quiet lies an intensely new and swarming world, so very different from the old one; and on the day that the forces of this underworld rise, we shall witness a complete reversal of our perspectives—secularism gloriously emerging from the womb of Iranian society.

I can tell you about the evolution of our ways because I know a thing or two about them. A few days ago, a meeting of sorts happened to be held at my place. A former employee of our company had come to see me for business; my faithful servant Hossein Agha was there too, and they both started talking about their children. They said young Iranians have dramatically changed their social attitudes: when they go out at night, they all wear ties and *pochettes,* drink alcohol without restraint, and dance to the rhythms of the latest Persian rap and techno music. Hossein Agha told me that when he asks his son why he adamantly insists on wearing a tie, while he himself never wore one, the young man replies: "When I wear a tie, I also need to wear a clean shirt and smoothly ironed pants—and I feel like a civilized man."

Those bleak moments are brightened sometimes by the presence of Afsaneh, who looks like a shooting star strayed among us. She visits us more frequently as of late; there is a lovely connection between us, except that we are not really on the same wavelength. She wants us to go away on a trip, or to live somewhere else—no matter where, so long as it is far from here; I feel that wherever we go, the sky, as the proverb says, will be of the same color. I am suffering from an exhaustion that seems as old as the history of my country, as if my blood were inhabited with all the epic failures of its memory.

Once she insisted, as she is wont to, that we leave this place as soon as possible, and she showed me a remarkably elaborate travel plan, complete with stops, halts, and detours. I told her, offhandedly: "Do you know how we differ from each other on this matter?"

"No," she answered, slightly taken aback.

"I am an old traveler, come home to the cradle after long trips around the world, while you are only starting your own odyssey; besides, I still bear the wounds of a vivid relationship, the outcome of which is far from conclusive."

"You mean Marianne?"

"Yes; she is always there, and as long as her presence endures, I will not be entirely free."

Well, there it is, dear Marianne; I leave it up to you to draw the conclusions, if any.

Tehran, April 21, 1999
Marianne, my dearest friend,

I went to the Caspian seaside with Afsaneh; my two friends Alireza and Jamchid also came along. We left by car, in these last days of April, driving on the old Chalous road. It's a climbing and winding road, which cuts through dizzying and steep passes over the abyss, through one hairpin bend after another, until it finally reaches the Kandivan tunnel. From there on, it plunges toward the sea, and the weather, all of a sudden, is surprisingly different: after the moonlike dryness of the heights, nature becomes more lush, even somewhat tropical. I have fond memories of this old road—when I was a child, I used to be dazzled by its proud summits; I would marvel at its awe-inspiring mountains appearing and disappearing in the snow and fog. All these images are so powerfully engraved in my mind that they form, as it were, like some intensely present vision, the topography of my soul. Once we arrived at Afsaneh's villa, we went for a walk by the seaside. The sky was cloudy and dull; the wind was blowing in gusts. I did not recognize the welcoming sea of my childhood; in its place, this sea has grown not only filthy and polluted but chillingly aggressive. It has reclaimed a dozen feet of land, ripping and carrying away everything in its wake. And no matter where we looked, we saw nothing but disemboweled houses, scattered junk, rubble torn off buildings. The old world that I had known was deeply disturbed—like the country itself—by the wrath of nature and men. As if, here, nature and men had lent one another a hand in destroying the inherent order of things.

We stayed for three days, doing nothing except chatting and making fun of everyone under the sky. This peculiar attitude we have adopted—which consists in deflating oppressive forms of seriousness that too often tyrannize us and looking at things the other way around so as to expose how grotesque they are—has become over time one of our very own specialties. With calculated complicity, we make use of all the weapons of deception: satire, irony, humor. People are taken aback, because they cannot tell whether we are in fact serious or facetious. Afsaneh fell right into the game. At first she was unsure; then she adjusted to the situation and proved so skillful at the art of sizing everything down to the absurd that we both rejoiced.

Afsaneh, who lived in America for many years, has a hard time adapting to the conditions of this country; she's at odds with its mores. So much seems wearisome and exhausting to her: donning the veil, coping with schizophrenic behavior, the double talk. In spite of her sense of humor and her scoffing at the political situation, she remains deeply honest and forward, and very American in her naiveté, in the way she appraises people. She wants to go back to the United States for a while, and she insists that I travel with her, if only for a short period. The idea of leaving Iran is thrilling, I must confess, because I've been immensely bored here for quite some time. But America is far away and I'm not sure I'll have the strength to undertake such a long trip, and above all, to throw myself once again into a world from which I feel so estranged. There was a time when the New Continent was a vigorous source of inspiration; I would draw from its arsenal of novelties, I would learn myriad enticing details, I would take, in a sense, the pulse of the world. Yet tired as I am, the mere thought of anything new frightens me, especially as I ponder that all new phenomena carry within themselves the seed of their own decay. How can I explain this to Afsaneh, who brims with the illusory wealth of the world? There I am, dear friend: in quite a predicament. From now on, I will be careful about dates. Why do I suddenly go back to the fifties in my previous letter? Because at that time, I still longed for the future.

Love.

A TASTE OF MY CINEMA
A Conversation with Abbas Kiarostami

Abbas Kiarostami is Iran's leading filmmaker and one of the most widely acclaimed directors on the international stage. Deftly thwarting censorship, his films conjure the poetry and longing of contemporary Iran. He has been awarded numerous prizes, among them the Palme d'Or at the Cannes International Film Festival for *Taste of Cherry* in 1997. His celebrated works include *Where Is the Friend's House?* (1987), *Close-Up* (1990), *Life and Nothing More...* (1992), *Under the Olive Trees* (1994), *The Wind Will Carry Us* (1999), and *Ten* (2002).

How did your adventure begin?

I was born in 1940 in Tehran to a large family. I was the first son. And like any other child—like my brothers, at any rate—my first interest was in drawing. But gradually, my interest grew more intense. So when I took my university entrance exams, I tried for dentistry and fine arts. I failed dentistry and made it to the School of Fine Arts, but in reality, I finished the drawing course with great difficulty. This course was supposed to take four years, and it took me no fewer than thirteen years to graduate! One reason was that I worked while I was studying, but mostly I was very incapable and untalented. Hence I gradually changed my specialty to making posters, graphic work for commercials, and credit titles for the cinema, and this is how I became acquainted with the mechanism of the camera. At the same time, I was invited to work on illustrating books for children, and I made a couple of books, which were not too successful. I wrote the stories as well, which weren't all that bad, since thankfully my writing was altogether better than my drawing... Then I founded the film department of the Institute for the Intellectual Development of Children and Young Adults, known as Kanun, and with the help of one of my friends, I began to make films for children. In 1970, I made my first short film, called *Bread and Alley,* a twelve-minute feature about a young boy who is sent to buy bread and walks back home. On his way, he catches sight of a dog on the street and, perhaps for the first time in his life, he is overwhelmed with fright—until he figures out how to get past this dog and reach his home. This was my first film.

What was your first film for adults?

If I am a good judge of my own work, I should say that all my subsequent films were more about children than for children. Everywhere in the world, children love comedies, fun, fantasies, cartoons...my films, from the beginning, were outside the scope of things children liked. Therefore I convinced myself that in our times, making films about children was more appropriate than making films for children, because it lent a certain consciousness to adults, it urged them to pay more attention to the world of children and enter another dimension, another form of understanding. The first film I created outside of Kanun was *Report* in 1977, but then I continued my films about children under the aegis of Kanun, even after the revolution. The institute saw the films after the audience did, so we were not censored. But after thirteen years working with Kanun, I had to quit because there occurred another revolution—a second revolution, so to speak. This was because in 1989 I made a film called *Homework,* about schoolchildren, and the film was regarded as problematic for the public education system.

How so?

Because it questioned the methods and system of education, and the Ministry of Education was not used to being criticized. So it reacted strongly against the film, myself, and the director of Kanun, and I was obliged to quit. By this time my own children had grown up, and I thought: the cycle of children has come to an end, and from now on I will work only with adults. Yet in this period, during those years I worked with children, I learned so much. The deceptive simplicity of their world, together with their acute sharpness, their libertine sense of playfulness—I thought I would keep all of that, borrow their gaze, as it were, behind my own camera, and bring it before the eyes of their elders.

What was the impetus behind *Homework*?
The film was about the lives of children after their school day is over, and it was somewhat under the influence of *Where Is the Friend's House?* It was about the problems that teachers create for children and about the helplessness of illiterate parents. So *Homework* brought together about thirty or forty children, who, just like the children of *Friend's House*, were all suffering from the lack of understanding and the insecurities of adults around them. It was the independent world of children as opposed to the dim world of adults, who were *not* guilty nonetheless, because they themselves lived in dreadful conditions after the war, both economically and socially.

Why did you decide to stay in Iran after the revolution? Was it actually a decision?
Around 1978, all the filmmakers lost their jobs for three or four years. There were no possibilities to make a film in the aftermath of the revolution . . . Cinema itself was in question: how was it going to evolve, and would it even survive? We did not have a thriving cinematic culture, thus we had to wait for cinema as a whole to be redefined, and we also had to absorb new information about the revolution. This was a time of hopelessness and despair. So, naturally, many of our colleagues decided to leave. As for myself, my luck or my curse was that during the same years I suffered from an internal revolution, which was separation from my wife. The responsibility for my two children was thrust upon

me—therefore I couldn't even think of leaving Iran or not. And when I look back on it now, I believe that this was one of the luckiest predicaments, that I didn't have the temptation to leave Iran. It was imposed on me by fate, and I stayed and adapted to the conditions and thought that I could continue my work.

The fact that you stayed in Iran and your love for the country: how do they affect the DNA of your films, so to speak? And what is your ideal interlocutor in Iran?

Without a doubt, my films are quintessentially Iranian: they speak of Iranian people, an Iranian is behind the camera, the language is Persian, the geography is Iranian, the social and daily issues are Iranian. Now, the question is that some people wonder whether these films have been made for an Iranian interlocutor. And here I must say that I simply make my films, and the films find their own viewers. Sometimes they happen to live in my neighborhood, sometimes they're in a different country altogether... For instance, with *Homework,* the first time I showed the film was at the Rotterdam film festival, and the reactions of the viewers were so powerful that I was certain at least half the audience was Iranian, but then when I asked, I realized that there was only one Iranian! Yet they had understood the film instant after instant, and one lady who came from South America cried and said that when she saw the film she was struck by the similarities to conditions in her own country. The education system the film had questioned didn't apply only to Iran but to many other countries as well. And this is one of many reasons why the societies of this world are so ill—because these very beings who are so innately astute and skittish are treated to extremely harsh conditions governed by egregiously wrong pedagogical principles. This, of course, makes them hopeless about continuing their education. In a word, I do not limit the interlocutors of my films to the geography of Iran. And if I did, I would be greatly mistaken. Because if we think of filmmaking as art, then for sure it needs to relate to variegated interlocutors in the global village. And in this context, any given Iranian viewer isn't intrinsically the best possible interlocutor for one of my films. In fact, I place contemporary Iranian viewers in several distinct categories. Those who are "America struck" and have seen too many American films and have expectations that they want to be entertained or stimulated by action—needless to say, my films simply don't do that. But as time goes by, I see that I can't really say that my fellow Iranians who are "enlightened" or intellectuals or art amateurs appreciate my work either. I have an architect friend, for instance, who knows art very well and is intelligent too, but he hates my films! He has told me that he'd sooner have dinner with his brother-in-law than buy a ticket to one of my films . . . On the other hand, I once met an illiterate Iranian woman who told me that time and time again, when all her children are in bed, she plays only two videos: one is *Maghshe Shab* (as she rendered *Mashghe Shab,* the Persian title of *Homework*) and the other is *Coolus-Up,* as she pronounced *Close-Up.* So I can't make social and intellectual generalizations and affirm that only "enlightened" people like my films. The people who like my films are those whose wavelengths are adapted to this cinema, and in the end it has nothing to do with their knowledge of art or how cultured they are.

Your cinema is permeated with poetry, and the structure of your films is essentially open. How does this affect the act of viewing?
The structure of my films *is* the structure of poetry . . . In schoolbooks, there were poems that enunciated a simple content through rhyme and rhythm—for me, those were not really poems. Many of them did not have an open ending, and they had obvious, straightforward conclusions. Poems, to my mind, are entities with open structures. These are more lasting, because readers can, according to the needs of their own interiority and self-awareness, their own reflections, elucidate the poem for themselves. And this directly relates to the information they have in their hands, not just to the information that is given to them. So in the realm of cinema as well, my belief is that a work cannot be too closed and that an open cinema is a more enduring

cinema, because it affords the possibility for viewers to find themselves and complete the film with their own imaginations. My artistic principle as a filmmaker, in a word, is that the structure of a film should remain open at all times, since it invites a constantly renewed dialogue between the "creation" and an indefinite number of "creators."

Is this the reason why there is also a great deal of quoted poetry in your films?

This has more do to with the culture I grew up in. In Iran, in conversation, the use of poetry is not limited to intellectuals, or poets, or even poetry lovers. We have simple people, illiterate people who, during the day, recite a couple of verses in order to relate to one another and express their viewpoints. Poetry in Iran pours down on us, like falling rain, and everyone takes part in it. Your grandmother, when she wanted to complain about the world—she complained with poetry. Or if she wanted to express her love for your grandfather, she expressed it with poetry, even faulty poetry... A while ago in Iran, for some reason, I went to visit an ancient bath, and there was a poem inscribed on the wall. It basically read: "Whosoever possesses an item of value, let him lend it to me at the door. Should he fail to do so and lose it, I shall not be held responsible." So this platitude one reads everywhere nowadays, they told it to us in the language of the poem, and this is actually a very old little poem. Because above all, poetry is the language of the Persian culture. Whether the poetry of Rumi or common poetry. Hence the use of poetry feels extremely natural to me in my films, whenever I want to follow the reality of everyday relations, simply because it's part of people's dialogues, or even of Iranians' monologues, when they wish to empty their hearts.

Do your films attract many spectators in Iran? And how difficult is it to see your films in the first place?

Unfortunately, it's quite difficult. From the time I began having a bit of success outside of Iran, my films have come under suspicion in my own country. When the "people in charge" watch them, they don't really grasp anything... Well, they do understand, but the films are so simple in a sense that they think: How could these films be so attractive to Westerners? They feel there must be something fishy, that there's some politics underneath them. Once I even heard the allegation that the West awards prizes to my films because they have no beginning and no end and thus artistically frustrate Muslim believers. And this pattern of thinking has turned into an epidemic. Many Iranians feel that these aren't really films in the classical sense. Administrators feel the same way and just don't see the point of showing my films in the cinema, so in the last ten years they have refrained from distributing my films altogether. The truth is: I don't have any complaints, because our society is struggling with problems that are far greater, to begin with. The economy, for instance, is in such a dire state that if we are somewhat realistic and lucid, we shouldn't whine about the fact that our films are not shown. Of course it's sad, but if I complain, it means that I don't know where I am living. When people are worried about their daily bread, who cares if they see my films or not. And for those who love cinema, two years after my films come out, they can purchase the video or the DVD for a much lower price than a film ticket, and they can see them in better conditions. For example, for my film *Ten,* the DVD was sold for 750 tomans (75¢), which means 250 tomans (25¢) cheaper than a cinema ticket, and people could lend it to one another, so that with one DVD, dozens of people could actually see the film. Therefore I don't think the government can ban our films or irrevocably censor us anymore. It can only punish, that is, arrange for no revenue of the film to ever find its way back to me, so that maybe I will no longer be able to make my films. But the era of banning has drawn to a close.

What is the current state of censorship in Iran?

Censorship, in reality, has now replaced outright banning. It is as though they had decreed: We will not ban, but we will censor.

For my film *Ten,* they simply asked me to remove half an hour of the final version. *The Wind Will Carry Us* had nothing for them to remove. So they said: Remove two verses by Forugh Farrokhzad. And I couldn't do that. It wasn't the poetry of Forugh with which they had problems, it was the sequence—they claimed it was pornography. While the poor girl was simply milking her cow, the boy was far away from her, and it was obvious that he was speaking with her—so even in the dark, there was no way he could take advantage of her or do much of anything. But no matter, because of these scenes, the film was banned and is still banned.

Weren't you able to show *Taste of Cherry* in Tehran?
Taste of Cherry, yes, because of all the justifying I did during that period. I explained to them that the film wasn't actually about suicide. In reality, my problems began after the award I received at Cannes. They just could not fathom how such a film, devoid of clear-cut dramatic intensity, could be awarded a prize of that caliber. So that became the perfect ground for misunderstanding the relationship between me and the "Western" audience. They imagined secret connections outside the film, bribery and what not...

I remember some years ago in Europe, regarding the films you made prior to *Taste of Cherry,* critics claimed you had chosen to work with children in order to thwart censorship. Was that true?
No, the children didn't have anything to do with it. Suffice it to look at my career. Until *Taste of Cherry,* my films received a few little prizes here and there, but they never really drew the regime's attention. The wind suddenly turned drastically with *Taste of Cherry.* Not so much because of the theme of suicide, but because they could not bear the idea that such a film could win the Palme d'Or. Before that, they had never meddled with my work.

But in this film, which represented a break from the "cycle of children," wasn't the notion of suicide eminently problematic for the Islamic Republic?

It still is a problem. But *Taste of Cherry* is visually so limpid that with the things I told the censors, I was able to justify that the film is not about suicide but about the essence of life, about the choice to live. And I don't know what happened in their minds, but they actually showed this film. They did manage, however, to punish me financially, because the person who distributed the film put its entire revenue in his pocket and ran away. The government, which had to back the rights of the producers, claimed it was none of its business, and thus no one defended me. This was their way of chastising me.

You were talking earlier about the poetic structure of your films. Doesn't this structure greatly complicate the task of the censors, which is to discriminate art in concrete, black-and-white terms? How could they even decide what to cut? It seems so strange and nonsensical, this confrontation between your vision and theirs...

The problem is that they don't even look at films in that way. They don't care about the structure at all. Perhaps the saddest moment for me was when they asked that I remove the verse by Khayyam in *The Wind Will Carry Us*. I told them I could not possibly do that and asked how they could even require this. Khayyam was, for so many centuries, the honor and pride of our nation, and now he should be censored! These lines are in all the books you never censored, I said. Countless times, you permitted the reprinting of his famed book of quatrains, the *Rubaiyat*—the book that is the most widely circulated and translated in the world, after the Gospel! So how could you allow yourselves to demand that I cut even one verse from Khayyam? In the end, just as with Forugh's poetry, we never reached an agreement. But again, please do not pay too much attention to my complaints. I am well aware that in the country in which I am living, the complaints of a filmmaker are too trivial to be heard. They seem almost indecent.

The novelty of your last film, *Tickets* (2005), which you directed in collaboration with Ermanno Olmi and Ken Loach, is that you chose to make it abroad. Suddenly you were able to show an unveiled teenage girl, a man and a woman interacting in the same sequence—in short, you could work without bothering about the gaze of the Islamic Republic. How did this impact your work?

The film followed its own principle, but the nature of my filmmaking didn't change. Naturally, the passengers of the train did not wear the *hejab,* because we made this film according to the geography and the mores of Europe. And needless to say, I did not import the self-censoring daemon I work with in Iran . . . If I had, I would need to visit the psychotherapist! When I came to Italy to make this film, I needed to feel this freedom, of course. But at the same time, I don't believe any major changes occurred. The passengers of the train dress as they do, just as we are able to see around us now, and no one stares at them. You know, more than the actual hejab, I feel that our problem in Iran is the "interior" hejab, which we haven't learned to don. Our people have not gotten accustomed to wearing the hejab in their minds and eyes, so instead they unload this responsibility onto others, namely women. Here, no one looks at these bare heads; here, they do not have the meaning they have in Iran, hence this film doesn't present any peculiarity as far as I'm concerned.

Do you ever tire of all the logistical problems, the political and religious issues that interfere with filmmaking in Iran?

No, I can't say that I do. I now fully understand the conditions in Iran and I know how to work my way around them. This film, *Tickets,* for instance, which was produced by the Italians, was the easiest film I ever made. In Iran, production is extremely complex and preproduction needs ten times more effort. Just to get close to producing a film, we need to stand in the rooms of bureaucrats who might understand next to nothing about cinema. Yet in spite of all this, I think I want to keep making my films in Iran. The experience with *Tickets* was decisive. When the time came to show this film at the Berlin festival, something incredible happened. Usually, when they show my films for the first time (and this is true of all filmmakers), my heart starts pounding for fear of a negative reaction. A director said in some interview that he always develops a fever, and I confess to a similar reaction. So for me, the strangest event when they showed *Tickets* in Berlin is that I suddenly realized that in the middle of my own film, I'd fallen asleep! And when I woke up, I began to wonder why. Why was the projection of this film not that exhilarating? As I thought about it, I became aware that, deep down, I did not believe this film was mine because I'd made it in collaboration with European directors, in Europe, and regarded it as a European film. Consequently I was very relaxed and even took a little nap... But this also carried a message for me: it's true that the film was successful in that it shattered linguistic and cultural barriers. At the same time, this was not my film because I wanted my film to speak Persian.

And when you are speaking your own language in a film, when you are showing your Iran, which is so drastically different from the Iran one sees in the daily news, are you aware of the fact that you are offering another face of Iran to the Western viewer?
Yes, without a doubt, my Iran bears little resemblance to the Iran that is portrayed in the daily news. And I have faith that my films are closer to the reality of Iran, that is, to its social, cultural, and spiritual heart. Foreigners who visit Iran, for instance, become incredibly attached to the Iranian spaces, the Iranian sense of relationships. I remember the first time the writer Jean-Claude Carrière came to Iran, he told me that he had traveled into the desert, and wherever he arrived at a home and asked, "Is there a guesthouse around here?" people said, "Please come in." And he went into these houses and found the contact with families and children was so natural it seemed like many travelers had passed by. "We came and stayed, and they laid their dinner on the floor for us, and I could not believe it," he told me. This is Iran. I can say it because I do a considerable amount of traveling, both for my films and for my work in photography. This is the reality of

kindness and hospitality. No matter how rudimentary the homes and how simple the people. And it is to this reality that my films speak, which is worlds apart from what is reported in the news media and from the unfortunate image that the government of Iran projects to the outside world.

Critics and filmmakers worldwide keep comparing you to a variety of Western directors—Fellini, for instance. Are there any filmmakers who have greatly influenced your visual language?

That's often the problem with journalists and critics: they think that if something is good, then it has to resemble something else or at the very least something greater. So this is a habit—when they wish to commend, they compare. They can't do without boxes, and they always have the possibility to remove a film from such and such a box if they find a more appropriate one later on. And since it is a habit, I can't take it very seriously. What is certain is that I have always been interested in the neorealists. Beyond that, I can hardly compare or judge my own films. Thirty or forty years need to pass, and if the film still lives on, if it has kept its sap as a work of art, then it's a good film.

How would you define vintage Kiarostami filmmaking?

First, there is the quintessential Iranianness of my films. I was born and grew up in Iran, I speak the Persian language, my knowledge is about Iran—so no matter what, my films are Iranian. Even *Tickets,* in spite of what I said earlier, I don't actually think it's entirely separate from my other films—at least not the segment of the film that is under my direction. If the space has changed, if some people feel that this film is not Iranian, well, the film's language is not Persian, but its cinematic language is my own. Without a doubt: the landscape shots, the storytelling, the open conclusion, the fact that we don't provide all the information to the viewer at the beginning. It's only in the middle and toward the end that the viewer finds out about the nature of the relationship between the boy and the woman. The style of the story is quintessentially Persian, it's the same style in which we observe our neighbors and then slowly absorb the information. This is not the way of contemporary cinema. The belief of most filmmakers today, and the signature of "classic" cinema at large, is that if you don't convey every single clue in the first ten minutes, your film immediately declines in intensity. In a word, your viewers know from the first minutes what is supposed to happen and why. Who is the Bad Man? Who is the Good Man? And who should judge them? In *Tickets,* we get gradually close to the passengers, and the viewers in the room have only as much information about this odd couple as the passengers on the train. My firm belief is that we cannot possibly narrate someone's life and determine, in the end, that we have said everything. Even when we want to borrow from reality, we cannot tell the whole story. So we must leave some things untold. And in the movie theater, the virtual prosecutors themselves, as they are signing their verdicts at the last minute, cannot think that they possess the definitive information about my characters.

You mentioned that the government of Iran had decided that the milking sequence in *The Wind Will Carry Us* was pornographic. At times, with contemporary American films, one feels that their full-disclosure ethos, their absolute predictability, is pornographic.

Yes, definitely, pornography is not limited to the genre itself. I feel that when we see a film about open-heart surgery, for instance, we see details that no one has the right to see—this is why they don't let us in the operating room in the first place. So to my mind this means that even in a film, I should not allow myself to show it. Pornography is not just sex. Pornography can also be the details of a relationship between a man and a woman, which they themselves can never see. For example, when you are kissing someone, when you are that close, you cannot actually see the person you're kissing, thus no one is witness to that scene. Why then should I become a witness to the scene through my camera? Pornography, I feel, is a wrong path that cinema has embarked on because of the range of possibilities offered by the lens. When the lens tells you: you can get this close to an object, it is entirely indifferent to the fact that in the telling of a story, you have your own limitations. In my opinion, you have no right to get so close to your subject, even if your lens permits you to. But most contemporary films get their graphic orders for action from the lens, not from reality. Their images are therefore naked and exposed, and I have no role in them as a viewer. I become useless.

Do you ever watch the latest Hollywood productions?
No, I haven't seen these films for years now.

Going back to your own films, is there any one that is closer to your heart?
No, some moments only. And they are the moments I haven't constructed, they are the moments that just happened. In this case, I like to get into my screening room, watch these moments, and come out again. But the shots I have constructed I have mastery over. And whatever you have mastery over no longer holds sway on you.

You are known for not working from full-fledged scenarios. So you begin with an idea, and then things slowly happen?
Yes, I have an idea, I say the dialogues. But everything is controlled. Sometimes, however, a moment occurs, nothing important. Sometimes, my actor bats his eyelashes twice, and I go into the screening room just to see those batting eyelashes and come out. And somehow, these batting eyelashes don't belong to me, and they don't belong to him either. I don't know, they're just a gift. And they are so timely and right that I keep wondering what happened for his face to express this reaction? There is a moment like this in the film *Ten* in the first seventeen minutes, with the boy in the car. It's always an object of marvel for me, because it's absolutely impossible to act these moments. So I simply observe and cherish them.

Would you like to say something about the film you are working on at the moment in Iran?

I prefer to wait. I want to see how this idea unravels, because at times I start off with a certain idea, I move toward it, and then realize that the idea I loved so much is destroyed and that other ideas have come to replace it. And perhaps it's far better for me to say nothing until the film is born—and we set eyes on what it is.

AN ALLEY GREENER THAN THE DREAM OF GOD

Babak Ebrahimian

"You cannot blame a nation for its government," Winston Churchill once remarked. From the media we gather nothing but demonic images of a totalitarian regime at work in Iran. Yet this perception is at once myopic and distorted in regard to *what* or *who* Iran and Iranians actually are. My proposition is that, perhaps, just as we look into a mirror to see an ever-changing reflection of ourselves, we should look, first and foremost, at the artistry of Iran's poems and films, the pulse and life of our nation. For poetry, more than any other art form, runs and beats in each Iranian's veins, while cinema has become the most celebrated and popular of our visual arts.

In the past two decades, the New Iranian Cinema has flourished to depict the life and times of contemporary Iran in a new and revitalized manner. Among the many writer-directors, Abbas Kiarostami has distinguished himself through a masterful combination of poetry and cinema that allows him to present variegated stories, commentary, and glimpses of Iran. One might argue, in fact, that Kiarostami has created a distinct "signature" based on poetry—a poetry of words, sounds, and images. His films have been compared to those of the Italian neorealist movement, mainly because they are shot on location with nonprofessional actors and offer a lining of social commentary. His films have also been compared to the cinematographic style of the Japanese grand master Akira Kurosawa; just as Kurosawa is admired for his slow-paced filming of landscapes, Kiarostami is said to be a director whose landscapes are deftly chosen and filmed to each second's precision. And in 1996, with his abrupt, self-conscious ending of *Taste of Cherry,* in which the final sequence has the cast and film crew suddenly turn up onscreen to a jazz soundtrack, Kiarostami came to be compared with the 1960s French New Wave. Yet, in spite of these similarities, Kiarostami's vision, in essence, retains an elemental Iranianness.

If every great filmmaker has a "secret" behind his or her films, then Kiarostami's secret lies in his careful multilayering of images and soundtrack. Sound, though not often noticed by the general audience, is as relevant as any visual sequence, and Kiarostami likes to run the entire gamut. The sound of a car grinding to a stop, the sound of footsteps on a gravel road, the sound of a boy weeping and insisting on returning his friend's notebook, the sound of animals in a village, and the peculiarly modern sounds of a cell phone—all are contained in the intricate universe of Kiarostami's vision. Where Kiarostami differs from other master directors is that he goes so far as to actually introduce and incorporate poetry as a layer of sound, and that this poetry soon takes on a life of its own within the film. Cohabiting with other sounds, the poetry quickly assumes a significant persona.

In his formative film *Where Is the Friend's House?* (1987), the very title is taken from "The Token," a poem by the contemporary poet Sohrab Sepehri. This poem is simple yet highly evocative, both abstract and concrete, and it mirrors the act of giving directions to another person:

> It was during the morning twilight that the rider asked: "Where is the friend's house?"
> The sky paused.
> The passerby lent the branch of light he held in his mouth to the darkness of the sands and pointed to the white poplar and said:
> "Before you get to the tree,
> There is an alley, greener than god's dream.

In it, love is as blue as the feather of truth.
Walk to the end of that alley
which emerges on the other side of maturity
and then make a turn toward the flower of loneliness,
two steps before this flower,
you'll arrive at the spring of Earth's eternal myths
and a transparent fright will take hold of you.
In the sincerity of the flowing space, you'll hear a rustle:
You'll see a child
who has climbed up a tall pine, to take a bird from the
    nest of light,
and you'll ask him
Where is the friend's house?"

The film closely follows the free style of the poem. A boy, Mohammad Reza, desperately wants to return his friend Nematzadeh's notebook, which he has accidentally brought home. This act of returning the notebook turns into a journey of following directions given to him by one person after another. We hear the boy repeat to his mother, "I must return it." The mother replies: "Do your homework," but Mohammad Reza appears quite determined and decides, regardless, to return the notebook. Here, at the onset of Mohammad Reza's journey in search of Nematzadeh's house, the music by Aman'allah Hossein starts and subtly announces and accentuates the journey as the boy zigzags up a hill, reaches the top, catches sight of a tree, then runs across the plains against the backdrop of the sky, down another hill, and through a landscape studded with trees. He finally arrives at a village, and the music stops just as he comes to a halt. In this sequence alone, we find the simplicity and boldness of Sepehri's poetry coming to life onscreen.

Now, having reached the village, the boy asks various people if they know where Nematzadeh's house is. A cow passes by through an alley. The boy continues to ask. A cat mews. He is finally provided a hint by a villager: the house of Nematzadeh's cousin has a blue door.

"Can you give me the address?"

"His house is at Khanevar. There is a staircase in the front and a blue door. The staircase is adjacent to the house."

"Which area?"

"Khanevar."

The directions are very much like the poem. Mohammad Reza knocks at the blue door and asks for his friend. A negative response is uttered. He returns exactly the same way he came. But while he is walking back to his village, the boy overhears a conversation and decides to follow a man on a donkey. The music is added once again to highlight the sequence as the journey proceeds. Mohammad Reza traces the man through alleys and up and down staircases. The man arrives at his home; a boy is standing at the door. A distraught Mohammad Reza begs him for directions:

"Do you know where the public bath is? The blacksmith's shop?"

"No, I come from Koker."

"Under their house they have a stable full of sheep."

"Which way?"

"This way." *(Pointing to the left)* "There is a dead tree next to their house."

It becomes apparent that Kiarostami is using directions as a poem, much like Sepehri in "The Token." Going beyond this recognition, we realize that not only do the directions act as a poem but that we, the spectators, are amid a carefully composed cinematic poem: landscape, dialogue, poetry, cries of animals, music are multilayered to conjure up sequence after sequence of montage. A visual journey gliding from one village to another, from friend to stranger. A bashful homage to the duties of friendship. The poem is limpid and so is the film, and Kiarostami's mastery lies precisely in this: he can take a straightforward poem, blow it up, and weave a dense and unique texture onscreen.

And the Wind Will Carry Us (1999), titled after a poem explored in the film, pushes the cinematic poetry even further. In this film, the poetry explores issues of life and death, light and darkness, and solitude. A group of filmmaking engineers arrives in a village, waiting to document the rites and rituals of the impending death of an old woman. As early as the opening of the film, we hear one of the engineers recite poetry while looking for the woman's address. The engineer exclaims: "Near the tree is a wooded lane greener than the dream of god." Thus words from Sohrab Sepehri's "The Token" are once again spoken at the beginning of a film. And the recited poem, along with the directions and the search—the journey of the engineers—remind us, of course, of *Where Is the Friend's House?* Meanwhile, the engineers are all guests at a house in the village, and a young boy acts as their guide. One engineer asks the boy why the village, which is so white in appearance, is named Black Valley. The engineer then begins to recite a poem, and the boy joins him: "When you're fated to be black / Even holy water cannot whiten you."

Impressed, the engineer asks how the boy knows the poem. The boy explains that each time the schoolteacher recites a poem, he learns it by heart. The film again affirms the role and importance of poetry, and Kiarostami shows poetry as a means of traditional bonding and communication between Iranians. Simultaneously, he mocks and shows the fragile limits of modern technology through the repeated breaking off of the engineer's cell phone reception, which requires higher elevation with each aborted call. Meanwhile, the ill woman does not die as expected, and the engineers eventually leave the premises. And poetry continues to envelop the film and its characters until the very last image. It penetrates every moment like a burning arrow.

We see Kiarostami at his best at the heart of this film. There is a long sequence of narrated poetry. Needing milk, an engineer visits another villager's house. The soundtrack in this scene begins with the milking of a cow, which is kept in the dark basement. A young girl is holding a faintly lit lantern. The engineer lends his metal pail to the girl, and we hear the sound of milk pouring in the pail. In spite of the lantern it is dark, and in this obscurity the sound of milking is followed by dialogue between the young girl and the engineer. This dialogue takes a sudden turn when the engineer asks the girl if he may recite a poem for her. At once, we are made to sense the multilayered poetics of the scene: the piercing sound of liquid falling into a tin pail along with a striking poem by the modern Iranian poet Forugh Farrokhzad, which echoes, illuminates, and supplements the visuals. The authentic exchange between the two characters begins with a poem and proceeds as follows:

If you come to my house
Oh kind one, bring me the lamp
and a window through which I can watch
the crowd in the happy street.
In my night, so brief, alas
The wind is about to meet the leaves.
My night so brief is filled
with devastating anguish.
Hark! Do you hear the whisper of the shadows?
This happiness feels foreign to me.
I am accustomed to despair.
. . . .
You, in your greenery,
Lay your hands
—those burning memories—
On my loving hands
And entrust your lips, replete with life's warmth
To the touch of my loving lips.

Girl: Your milk is ready.
Engineer (continues): The wind will carry us.
Girl: Your milk is ready.
Engineer: Yes, yes, The wind will carry us!

Completing his recital, the engineer continues to echo the language of the poem: "Raise the lantern so I can see your face ... You won't tell me your name and you won't let me see your face. At least light the ground so I don't stumble." Tradition holds strong, and the girl lights the ground. Yet she asks about Forugh the poet ...

Embedded in the soundtrack are other sounds of the farm animals and the village. Thus visual and auditory poetry become one in Kiarostami's language. They not only echo one another but they also play off each other. And the presence of poetry does not end in this scene but it carries on, just as the girl asks about the young Forugh. The beginning of the film hinted at poetry and Kiarostami fulfills his promise, with the audio and visual tracks working together to create a demurely lyrical montage. The engineer emerges from the dark basement, his pail filled with milk; the inhabitants of the house do not charge him for the milk but rather insist on the fact that he is a "guest"—an ancient tradition of Iranian culture, known as *tarrof,* in which the guest or visitor is accorded the highest respect and honor.

Finally, in one of the last scenes, we find the engineer riding on the back of the doctor's motorcycle—riding through green landscapes. They are in the midst of a conversation in which poetry, once more, enhances and completes the visuals.

> *Engineer*: Old age is a terrible illness, doctor.
> *Doctor*: Yes, but there are worse illnesses. Like death ...
> *Engineer*: Death?
> *Doctor*: Yes. Death is the worst. When you close your eyes on this world, this beauty, the wonders of nature and the generosity of God, it means you'll never be coming back.
> *Engineer*: They say that the other world is more beautiful.
> *Doctor*: But ... who has come back from there to tell us if it is beautiful or not?
> They tell me she is as beautiful as a *houri* from heaven!
> Yet I say that the juice of the vine is better.

Prefer the present to these fine promises.
Even a drum sounds melodious from afar...
Prefer the present...

Ending the ride with a poem by Omar Khayyam, the engineer reaches the village and takes a snapshot of the mourning procession. The old woman has just died. The film starts and ends with poetry, asserting yet again that between poetry and cinema the gap is tenuous, perhaps even irrelevant. Kiarostami begins with an aesthetic epiphany and then elaborates on it, pushing the limits and boundaries of narrative cinema, and crafting unexpected definitions and directions. In the darkness of our screening rooms, it is then up to us to raise our minute lanterns and open the dialogue.

DON'T CRY FOR ME, AMERICA

Negar Azimi

Never having set foot in Tehran, one could judge it unlikely that the country that seems to elicit periodic alarm on the nightly news would also be home to punk rock, transvestites, and reality television. This is what might be termed first-level unawareness, the standard axis-of-evil vision trumpeted by the conservative media and celebrated in a glib fashion that tends to present Iran in anachronistic, stark, absolutist terms. In short, all that we accept as familiar in the West is presented as inimical to the spirit of the Islamic Republic. Second-level unawareness is only a tad more realistic. Its worldview of Iran is marked by certain canonical images: the ubiquitous nose job, the skintight hejab, the bumbling mullah, art-house cinema, and beyond. Where contemporary art production fits into these dominant cultural paradigms is not immediately evident, but what is certain is that Iran is in the midst of an unprecedented movement in the arts—one that radically challenges our notions of what art making in that part of the world may be.

Iranian artists today are producing works that defy the pigeonhole, testifying to a new generation's ingenuity and moving past what some critics have coined the "poornographic" realm of arts production—that is, the circulation of images and ideas that tend to perpetuate the image of a victimized people. Prominent among these ideas is the notion that Iran is a sealed vacuum of repression and, therefore, that any art production emanating from within its bounds is a hysterical reaction to that reality, in other words, *cry for us because our fates are so bad.* In fact, there is no reason to lament; Iranian visual arts have been thriving, particularly in the last decade. While inevitably linked to the excesses of the current regime, the arts also remain quite independent of them —a testament to a persistent originality and a remarkable renegotiation of prevailing status quos.

Beyond a long and distinguished history of drawing, painting, and sculpture, the camera also has a particular relationship to the country—one that has seldom drawn attention. Indeed, contrary to its regional neighbors, Iran has rarely proclaimed bans on representation (while Egypt's Al Azhar mosque has issued fatwas against photography, one of Iran's 2005 presidential candidates, Hashemi Rafsanjani, appointed a filmmaker, Kamal Tabrizi, the brain behind the controversial hit film *The Lizard,* as one of his campaign managers). Only a year after the camera's invention in the middle of the nineteenth century, the first of such objects made its way into the hands of a curious Qajar ruler. Though it remained an aristocratic enterprise throughout the Qajar era, the Constitutional Revolution of 1906 and the advent of Reza Shah in 1925 popularized the medium, as evidenced by its rapid adoption by the bourgeoisie. Reza Shah, for his part, recognized that he could institutionalize his reign by impressing his visage on all manner of postage stamps and official documents. Meanwhile, his decree that all citizens must have an identity certificate *(shenasnameh)* set the scene for most Iranians' debut encounter with the camera. Reza Shah's reign would also be Iran's first experiment with state-sponsored photojournalism. Years later, his son Mohammad Reza Shah's use of images presented a ruler at the helm of an Iranian state on the cusp of modernity—with a decidedly Western sheen.

Fast-forward five decades: the architects of the 1979 revolution in turn were quick to recognize the latent power of images. Officially sanctioned war documentaries *(revayat-e fath),* ubiquitous wall murals lionizing fallen martyrs (blurring the lines between the landmark Shiite martyrdom of Imam Hussein in the seventh century and the ten-year war against Iraq), and museums dedicated to the memory of war veterans each reveal the use of visual arts as an effective tool in consolidating popular support, scripting history, and exporting myths en masse.

The late shah's wife, Queen Farah, was known for her unusually modern taste in art, most memorably manifest in the Shiraz Festivals of the 1970s, which brought to the ancient city of Shiraz artists such as John Cage, Jerzy Grotowski, Robert Wilson, and Merce Cunningham. Needless to say, the queen left a vivid legacy. Her distinctly avant-garde leaning coupled with her collecting zeal produced a national treasure trove—impressive works that sit to this day in the basement of the Tehran Museum of Contemporary Art. Though most works remain hidden away from the public, the collection never fails to inspire intrigue and a conspiracy theory or two—from burned Hockneys to Picassos sold on the sly.

Following the revolution and the downfall of the Pahlavi dynasty, official art patronage moved away from its blue-chip Western tendencies, arguably turning inward. Some might even suggest that art died, placed on hold until it could be cleansed by the cultural revolution. Painting biennials were graced with the prefix "Islamic," and "good" art became intimately linked to ideals tied to the doctrines of the revolution. The Iran-Iraq war that came on its heels signaled the closing of the museum and its use as a nursing home for the wounded men of the front. Some especially dedicated staff members moved into the museum, spending nights there to guarantee that the collection remained safe. Nevertheless, it was clear by then that the tide had turned, and that the days of a hip queen's euphoric patronage of the arts had drawn to a close.

While the revolution put a freeze on contemporary arts, the war gave birth to a new generation of photographers. As thousands of young men volunteered to go to the front, many of them traveled with mini Kodaks, Minoltas, and Canons in hand. Here, photography reached new ritualistic heights, as having one's portrait snapped became a rite of passage for most young men on the war front—often in anticipation of imminent death. A decade later, these portraits of the deceased, some amateur and others shot in studios around the country, dot the graves of thousands assembled at the city's sprawling Behesht-e Zahra cemetery in a seductive, color-tinted vision of the country's fallen. And this is to say nothing of the abundance of photojournalistic work carried out during both the revolution and the war. We now know the names of many of the photographers who worked during those years—Abbas, Bahman Jalali, Rana Javadi, Kaveh Kazemi, Seifollah Samadian, and the late Kaveh Golestan, among many others. Not only have these photographers created their own vast bodies of work, they have also served as mentors and teachers to the next generation of Iranian image makers.

Today, the legacy of this awesome visual culture is striking. While the press routinely cites the preponderance of anxious, discontented youth under the age of thirty, less is said about the subcultures they have spawned. For many, the Internet has evolved into an unparalleled venue for the arts—photographic and otherwise. From the simple cataloguing of artists' work to original commissions presented through photo blogs, the Internet arguably starts to level the playing field, providing a platform for work that would likely be barred from exposure at home given prevailing concerns about un-Islamic representation in the eyes of the official arts establishment and its censors. Equally, the Internet provides a platform for exposure abroad—which is crucial, given the difficulty young people often have in securing visas, let alone in networking with outside curators. Twenty-four-year-old Amir Ali Ghasemi, for instance, recently graduated from Azad University's art school and has been hosting an online gallery, the Parking Gallery, since 2002. As a physical parallel to the virtual gallery, Ghasemi now also holds self-initiated, self-funded, and self-curated exhibitions in the garage of his parents' home. He has hosted some thirty-four young artists on his Website and even larger numbers in actual exhibitions within the parking area. When an exhibition is shut down in Tehran, it is not uncommon for it to find its way either to Ghasemi's Website or, alternatively, to the concrete home afforded by the garage.

And beyond Ghasemi's Internet site, there are numerous others that serve as forums for the arts, from TehranAvenue to Fanoos Photo.

While there is a tendency to fetishize the historic division between public and private space in Iran (traditionally referred to as *biruni* and *andaruni*)—a division that seemed accentuated in the aftermath of the revolution and the codes it generated regarding conduct in public space—visual artists within Iran have found creative ways to turn these rigid codes on their heads. Artists Farid Djahangir, Bita Fayyazi, Atta Hasheminejad, Khosrow Hassanzadeh, and Sassan Nassiri joined forces in 1998 to convert an abandoned home situated near the Hosseinieh Ershad mosque (incidentally, the site of the Ministry of Culture) into a studio-gallery. The reaction to the initiative was tremendous, as hundreds of Tehranis flocked to visit the space. The fact that this space and the work within were eventually razed in order to accommodate an impending high-rise seemed almost incidental while filmmaker Maziar Bahari recorded the events in his *Honar-e Takhrib (Art of Demolition)*. Bita Fayyazi, for her part, has been a pioneer in the realm of public art projects. In 1997, she lay 150 terracotta dogs on a stretch of empty road near Tehran. Looking as though they had been crushed, the dogs made up an installation (created in collaboration with Mostafa Dashti) titled *Road Kill*. The dogs' subsequent burial in a mass grave and the construction of yet another high-rise on that very site has since been documented on video as well.

In the spring of 2004, an enterprising young sculptor named Mahmoud Bakhshi-Moakhar placed thirty sculpted arms, flexed in a revolutionary pose, in the central mosque of the bazaar of Tehran—a focal point of the revolution and arguably one of the most symbolically loaded sites of the city. The artist's message of revolt seemed evident but, camouflaged as support for the current regime, it managed to seduce the authorities as a sufficiently respectful, even reverent, installation before it was shut down a number of days later. Months earlier, the duo of Shahab Fotouhi and Neda Razavipour took over the empty spaces of the Atisaz building, a modernist megalith off Tehran's Chamran Highway, in a project titled *Census.* Seventy backlit photographic portraits of young people occupied the building in a subtle statement about access to public space and freedom of expression.

And so contemporary Iranian artists are facing up to their own realities rather than others' imagined "poornographic" realities. The poornographic captures the essence of an imagined postrevolutionary Iran marked by stringent censorship. It is pervaded with aesthetic expression that tends to privilege the countryside over the city and marked by a symbolism that sometimes hits you over the head, generally emphasizing the preconceptions that you may have about Iran from the perspective of, say, New York or Paris.

While the temptation to produce work that caters to an external art market bent on consuming exotica of the "poornographic" variety is palpable, many contemporary artists are defying these tendencies. Hassanzadeh's silk-screen homage to nine prostitutes murdered by a fanatic in Mashhad in 2001, Solmaz Shahbazi's dialogue with Tehrani youths in the documentary *Good Times/Bad Times,* Bahman Kiarostami's film work on the ritualistic crying of professional mourners in *Tabaki,* Ghazel's slapstick videos, and Marjane Satrapi's graphic novellas about her childhood and adolescence in postrevolutionary Iran are all visual odes to these creative tendencies and their ability to overcome raging clichés. Though the elder Kiarostami, Abbas, is undeniably a master auteur, his cinema is by no means indicative of current trends in domestic production or consumption. One can in fact argue that modern Iranian film is more often about the "present-day" concerns of sex, drugs, and depression than about imaginative ways to overcome censorship or repression— effectively closer to Hollywood than Cannes in both style and substance.

Farhad Moshiri and Shirin Aliabadi take on clichés surrounding Iran as the point of departure in their body of work. At first glance, the duo's work seems a monument to third world kitsch: upholstered truck interiors, vernacular street photography, plates featuring printed photographic images. On closer inspection, however, the subversive nature of their approach becomes apparent, exposing the tendency to commodify exotica. The pair's packaged chadors and faux soap operas are both hysterically funny and damning. Moshiri's photographs of north Tehran apartment facades and hypergilded furnishings turn the jokes on Iranians themselves, acknowledging their own complicity in rendering themselves packaged products, tending to privilege the language of surfaces and the baroque.

Like Aliabadi and Moshiri, the Zurich-based artist Shirana Shahbazi is also aware of the tropes associated with an imagined Iranianness. Her photographic works capitalize on the baggage we bring to the table as viewers when confronted with images of Iran—or Shanghai, for that matter. Shahbazi is demanding—particularly at a time in which the majority of our encounters with images are incidental and shallow, mediated through slogans and pop icons. She knows attention spans are short and focuses on the fixed manner in which we consume the world around us. The seductive glance of an attractive blonde, a city skyline, a landscape, a bride, a stadium. Delivered in iconic slick packaging, her photographs reek of monumentalism. Nevertheless, our grandiose expectations are rejected; the author of these images continually trumps these expectations, exposing the danger of the cursory glance. The promise of easy climax is never fulfilled as Shahbazi captures the quotidian. A portrait of a veiled woman, for example, is sexy and provocative in principle, but a closer look reveals that the subject is not even looking at the camera. The promise of the cliché is aborted: children play in the park, a pharmacist scans the stockroom. But while anticlimactic in a sense, these images are delivered in the form of technically superior prints, often large in format. Their crispness and clarity seem at odds with a content that is neither stylized nor cinematic. In an exhibition context, Shahbazi will frequently interrupt her own photographs with photographs of landscapes, still lifes, portraits —a self-conscious selection that spans the breadth of art history. In this, she emphasizes the manner in which we read images, enlightening us as to our own visually reductive tendencies and expectations given particular "packaging"—and hence the bias we bring to every visual encounter. Her message is a fundamentally destabilizing one, her art especially intelligent.

Beyond the handful of Iranian artists mentioned here, there are innumerable more. And with each passing month, new art magazines, galleries, artist Websites and blogs are launched in the concrete capital that is Tehran and in cities throughout the country. The pace of activity is dizzying. These original movements, while often hidden from the wider art-consuming public, testify to the fact that with Iran, we must ultimately leave our tidy preconceptions at the door. And this is just the beginning.

WHY ACTING SET ME FREE

A Conversation with Shohreh Aghdashloo

Shohreh Aghdashloo became internationally recognized after earning an Oscar nomination for her role in *House of Sand and Fog* in 2003. Known for her resounding beauty, character, and political beliefs, Aghdashloo began her career in Iran in the early 1970s. She fled the country at the time of the Islamic revolution and started over, first in England, then in America, with both cinema and stage work.

How did you become an actress in Iran? And what was your first role like?
I started my career at the Drama Workshop of Tehran in 1973. This workshop consisted of small groups of devoted actors, playwrights, directors, and producers who were among the elite society of intellectuals and freethinkers of the day. It was a theater company that produced and performed works of the great international playwrights—a majority of them Western but translated into Farsi—as well as original Iranian plays. It was a unique platform for young artists. I was fortunate in that my very first role was the lead in *The Narrow Road to the Deep North,* a play by Edward Bond. This came about after a long process of auditions, at which time I also became a member of this prestigious workshop.

Was it difficult to become an actress in Iran? Did your family disapprove?
Yes, as a matter of fact, it was rather difficult. My huge obstacles were my parents, my family's good name, and my obligations as an Iranian daughter. It was my parents' wish that, along with my

brothers, I pursue a higher education abroad—anything, basically, but become an actress. As a teenager growing up in Iran, however, my overwhelming desire to be an actress left me no choice but to follow my own path. Therefore, since there were already a few suitors asking for my hand, I announced to my shocked parents that I preferred marriage to a higher education. Perhaps, in my young mind, I thought it possible that my knight in shining armor, riding his white horse, would come and ask for my hand and set me free so that I could follow my heart. By an extraordinary twist of fate, my prayers were answered, and one day he walked into my life—a bright and talented artist. When I asked him: "If I were to marry you, could I be an actress?" he looked into my eyes and said: "I do not see why not."

What was your most memorable role in Iran?

The portrayal of a young prostitute in *Souteh Delan (Broken Hearts),* a film by the late Iranian filmmaker Ali Hatami. I was extremely taken with the grace of this character when I first read the script: an adolescent girl is victimized by her society and forced into prostitution. She then falls in love with a retarded young man. Before long, there were a few fiercely negative voices against my portrayal of a prostitute. I was fully aware of the consequences and made the choice nonetheless. Today, this film is considered one of the classics of Iranian cinema.

When did you leave Iran?

Demonstrations had spread throughout the streets in all the cities of the country. Driving though the crowds of mostly young people chanting in unison, "Khomeini rahbar, Alaho akbar" (God is great, Khomeini is our leader) was as macabre as reading *The Trial* by Franz Kafka, only this time a nation was being tried by its own youth. They were demanding the fall of the shah's dynasty and the return of Khomeini. Naively, they believed the ayatollah would be their Gandhi. Time and history proved them wrong.

It was 4:30 a.m. on February 28, 1979. I started my journey to the West in the company of two friends. I left with a few articles of clothing and personal belongings, just enough for a short trip. I also took a few photographs of my family and of my early years in theater and cinema along with two of my favorite theater costumes, which I had worn as my characters in Mishima and Strindberg productions. Driving thirty miles an hour, it took us seven days to reach the Turkish border. The scene at the border was chaotic. We all knew the airports had been shut down. Thousands of cars, bumper to bumper, were filled with Iranians desperately trying to flee their country. Claiming we were on our way to a vacation in Turkey, we somehow made it across the border and into Turkish territory. How can one ever forget a scene that so peculiarly resembled the border sequence in the novel and film *The Unbearable Lightness of Being*?

Once in Turkey, we embarked on our journey to Yugoslavia, then to Venice. From Venice, we drove through the South of France and Paris until we reached London. The entire trip took us thirty-one days. I remember that when I set foot in London, all I could think of were the words "freedom" and "democracy."

Was it difficult to take up acting abroad?

Ironically, when I left Iran, I had decided to study politics. I received my BA in international relations in 1983 in England. I was convinced that I had left my acting career behind in Tehran, but this was not to be my fate. Following the graduation ceremony, an old friend, an Iranian playwright named Parviz Kardan, suggested that now that I was free to do as I pleased outside Iran, I should take a look at a play he had written—with a lead in it for me. Although I had decided I did not want to act anymore, the actress in me whispered the temptation: "Come on, now, read it."

It is the story of an Iranian man who has fled to England after being accused of having served in the shah's fearsome SAVAK intelligence agency. He flees in order to save his life and reside in a peaceful country but cannot tolerate witnessing the destruction of his homeland by a new regime, even from a distance.

Therefore, to make a political statement, he decides to commit suicide at the residence of Sudabeh, the character I ultimately played. Sudabeh is a wealthy Iranian widower living in a lavish seventeenth-floor flat by the river Thames. And this man has planned it all, hoping that jumping out of Sudabeh's window with a note in his pocket will compel the Western media to shed light on the brutality and injustices at work in Iran. But Sudabeh convinces him to stay alive and write a lot more than just a note —sharing his story, she argues, would have a far greater impact on Iranian politics than ending his life ever could.

I loved the play and decided that perhaps I, too, could do more by staying alive as an actress and bringing this story to existence on the stage. In the end, it was this decision that brought me to the film *House of Sand and Fog* twenty years later.

What has been your most outstanding role in America to this day?

It most definitely has to be Nadi Behrani in *House of Sand and Fog,* a book by Andre Dubus III brilliantly adapted to the screen by director Vadim Perelman. It's the portrayal of a voiceless woman, trapped in a web of tragic circumstances brought about by her family's migration to a new land—America.

What did it feel like being nominated for the Oscar for best supporting actress in *House of Sand and Fog*?

I was elated. It was an immense, and almost unbelievable, honor to be acknowledged by the Film Academy and to be nominated among such talented American actors whose work I had admired for years. What can I say? It was the ultimate reward. Sheer happiness...

Beyond the obvious prestige, did it also have a symbolic value in your eyes, as an Iranian woman?

Yes, it was the realization of my overwhelming desire—when I left Iran—to pursue my dreams as a free being in a free society. It also meant that I had acquired a voice as a woman, and that was extremely symbolic to me. I hoped it would send a message to the millions of talented and intelligent women in Iran: that if it could happen to me, then it could happen to them.

On another note, do you feel you are necessarily typecast as an Iranian?
Other than the role of Nadi Behrani in *House of Sand and Fog,* which called for an Iranian actress to play the character, I have been offered and performed characters of many different ethnicities. I believe an actor has endless faces, and with the help of today's makeup techniques and technology, no actor should be limited.

Are your acting choices intrinsically political choices?
My presence here in the United States is of a political nature, therefore my professional choices are, indeed, intrinsically political. It was the pursuit of freedom and democracy that brought me to this vast and generous country, and every character I play speaks, whether onscreen or onstage, to the freedom of choice that is the very principle of my existence as an Iranian woman émigré.

You recently played the part of a female terrorist. Was she an Iranian? And what was your motivation behind this choice?
Contrary to what many believe, the character of Dina Araz in the drama series *24* was not Iranian. In fact, the family's nationality is never revealed, and I should hope that the audience would look beyond my ethnicity. As for the motivation, I was attracted to this role and challenged to portray a multidimensional and complex character. As an actress, I was most challenged to grasp the psyche of a female terrorist who is also a loving mother.

What have been some of your other "political" roles in recent years?
Of course, being married to a writer, my second husband, secured me the lead in all his plays . . . ! One such role was the portrayal of a Westernized Iranian American wife in the play titled

Sweet Scent of Love, which debuted in 1990 and wrapped in 1994 after more than a thousand performances worldwide. I had the formidable task of becoming Afsaneh, a free-spirited, freedom-seeking creature, somewhat stuck in the 1960s feminist mind-set, who, along with her male and very gay best friend, is on a quest to free Iran through her volunteer work with the United Nations. But Afsaneh is married to Jamshid who, for his part, is adamant about escaping the reality of his Iranian past. This gap in their worldviews has brought them to the edge and on their way to a divorce, when suddenly Afsaneh's old uncle decides to visit them from Iran. This, of course, puts their divorce plans on hold in order to save face in front of their families back in Iran. But gradually, the arrival of the uncle, who has brought with him a piece of both Afsaneh's and Jamshid's past, conjures up memories of who they were...and a newfound sense of who they actually are, down to their roots. The play was a masterpiece of writing—the perfect melange of melancholy and comedy —and it was a brilliant way to encourage the audience to reflect on its own origins. Four years and a thousand performances later, I must say that Afsaneh contributed to my reconnecting with Iran as well, and through her, I became more the woman I am today.

Is reconnecting with Iran the reason you chose to act in Shirin Neshat's art films?

I had always admired Shirin Neshat's enlightened sense of film-making, and I was very pleased to be involved in two of her films. For me, this was the ideal opportunity to lend a face to the forgotten souls of women banished by Iranian society. I played the roles of women driven mad by loneliness and ostracism, and gave life to their pain and their beauty. To me, this was a political as well as an artistic statement—that casting these women away from the gaze of society does not annihilate them and that through everything they have endured, they have remained the beating heart of Iran.

Do you feel that you are in any way a goodwill ambassador for the image of Iran abroad? Or at the very least in America?

In an era in which many Iranians have achieved impossible dreams around the world, I am indeed honored if, through my work, I have become part of a movement—that is to say, in my case, a platform—where our voices, as free Iranians, can at last be heard.

Are you in touch with men and women inside Iran?

I am afraid that, as of this date, I am not able to return to Iran, but I am grateful that the people of Iran have not forgotten me. I follow the country's current affairs and read any available books and newspapers I can get my hands on. I also make sure I don't miss the latest work of artists and filmmakers. Mostly, I receive news from relatives and visiting friends.

What do you think of Iranian cinema today?

The Iranian films that I have seen in recent years—such as *Rain* by Majid Majidi, or *Under the Olive Trees* by Abbas Kiarostami— are not only internationally acclaimed, they also represent a generation of talented, dedicated, and responsible filmmakers. These filmmakers hold the keys to our identity, not the politicians in power.

What is your dream for Iran?

To see Iran FREE.

TEHRAN UNDERGROUND

Salar Abdoh

"Why do you want to know about the snow?"

I hadn't seen Ziba in almost a year, and she had grown even warier of anyone traveling from abroad to write yet *another* story about Iranian lives. Being a paid tourist was what she called it.

"But I only want to know about the snow," I said.

It had been one of those memorable winters. Tehran, a city not known for the wonders of its sights, covered for weeks on end with ever-replenishing piles of fresh white snow. People had taken it as an omen. It hadn't snowed like this in years. Maybe change was in the air. Maybe the Americans were finally coming. Or the mullahs had simply decided to skip town while they still could. This was a lot of wishful thinking, of course, and there had been so much of it in the past quarter century. The Americans might come one day, but it was unlikely the mullahs would surrender that easily. And who was to say that everyone wanted the mullahs to leave anyhow? After all, the milieu that Ziba and I came from knew Iran mostly through negation. This meant confining ourselves to the wealthier northern parts of the capital and to each other's homes. It meant not exactly rebellion against the Islamic Republic but casual disdain for it—the kind that allows one to conveniently shut oneself in and lead an utterly detached existence from the life of the swamp. For Tehran's traffic has made the place exactly that, a swamp where movement is enormously difficult; one simply doesn't move much if one doesn't need to. And barely two days into my eight-day stay, I was already feeling the thrust of an all too familiar indolence creeping in. Originally, anticipating a summer research grant from my university, I'd flown from New York in the middle of the teaching season to get some preliminary ideas about Iranian attitudes toward a possible U.S. invasion. I'd thought that perhaps the idea of the snow and what it portended would be a roughly clever way to segue into the subject. But the idea already exhausted me, because Tehran did. I couldn't possibly begin to do any serious research unless I got out to the provinces, and eight days were simply not enough for that kind of work. I'd have to come back in the summer, with the hope that no invasion had taken place just yet, or I might have to give up the grant money.

In the meantime, I sought out Ziba, who was nearly always in a bad mood since returning to Iran. But being in a bad mood was a luxury my friend could afford. She had an American passport and could fly to the United States whenever life in Tehran got too unbearable. I would have liked to point this out to her. I suppose I also wanted to somehow prove I hadn't come to write just an exotic, sob-story piece about the East or about terrorists or about Islam. I asked her how it was for her these days, working in the Iranian film industry. She shrugged. "Like everything else, it's a mirage." When I asked what she meant by that, she ran her thin fingers through her dyed auburn hair and offered something even vaguer: "It's like the snow: here today, gone tomorrow."

"What do you mean?"

"You can't sink your teeth into anything here," she said, suddenly switching to English. "I might make a film this year and the censors might okay it. I might make the same film next year and they might not. It's like walking on air. What it's really like is the snow. And you can't build a house made of snow."

Giving up on Ziba then, the next morning I called Nina, who nervously asked for the number of the home I was staying at before briskly hanging up. Nina was another returnee from the States, having come back to try and reclaim the numerous properties the revolution had taken from her family. This meant that the last seven years of her life she'd spent mostly chasing her own tail, leaping from one messy intrigue to another without ever actually getting closer to recouping her family's loss. "I import clothes now," she explained when she finally called back. Apparently, the man she did the importing with was a "heavy" in the government. He needed her language skills for overseas business, and she needed his money and contacts. They'd entered a *sigheh,* a temporary marriage contract—even though the man was already married—so they could be intimate with each other. "He thinks he's still religious. That's why I can't talk to you from my own house." There was a pause, then she said, sighing, "I'm bored to death because of this guy. I haven't been to one single party in the last three months." I explained to her that this was precisely why I'd called. I needed a party. "A party for what? Research?"

No, I said, skipping over my grant proposal and the theme of snow, telling her instead about the living room of my relative who was putting me up for the week. There was a television in that living room. And in the past couple of days, I'd come to think that this particular television, which was just about always turned on, was dedicated solely to pornography. This in itself was nothing new; through hidden dish antennas many households could now watch the entire range of forbidden European satellite channels. But what had struck me this morning was the following: with cunnilingus in full swing on the twenty-six-inch screen, the fairly devout-looking cleaning lady placidly went about her business of sweeping the living room floor, as if nothing out of the ordinary were happening in her work space. And perhaps it wasn't; except that this was still the Islamic Republic, and that the juxtaposition of the veiled lady sweeping on the one hand and the pornography on the other seemed slightly fantastic to my eye.

"So what?" Nina responded to what I'd just described. "If you want the *Thousand and One Nights,* don't bother reading about it, just come to Tehran and you'll see what you need to see."

That whole *Thousand and One Nights* comparison was used up, I told her. A daft romanticization of the glum nights of Tehran. I wasn't interested in it. What interested me was how the Iran my relatives lived in seemed so entirely removed from the Iran of the cleaning lady I'd seen this morning. Mutually exclusive lives, abstracted from and invisible to each other. And if the Americans wished to invade this place one day, which of these characters would they lend their ears to? Which one would they believe represented the true Iran?

I had no doubt that Nina knew where all the parties were, even though she was currently engaged with her government-sanctioned "religious guy." And when she groaned and claimed that she hadn't been to a party in three months, what she really meant was how desperately cut off she was from the pulse of her town. Why? Because in a country where the public display of pleasure is not only frowned upon but punishable, life behind closed doors can become the only life that carries some substance. I felt I needed a new read on those closed doors because, like my relative's illegal TV antenna, they represented an alternate dimension to the heart of the Iranian capital.

So I waited. Nina had said she'd get back to me as soon as she found out about something really exciting. But after another day and night had passed with no word from her, I began to worry that perhaps Nina, like Ziba, had decided she'd had enough of people who descended on her city for a quick tour and an article.

The call, however, finally came. I was to take the "Telephone Taxi" service to a flower shop in the Shahrak-e Gharb neighborhood. There, I'd wait on the street for my ride. My ride turned out to be a white Peugeot occupied by a young man in the back and two more in front. They were a happy bunch who good-naturedly asked me to lower my head a bit, hostage style, and not look up until they told me I could. Ten minutes and a half-dozen turns later, three of us, minus the driver, got out in front of a large, yellow brick house. I'd been to my share of Tehran parties before and didn't at first understand all the fuss. I asked one of the fellows why we were going to a party at one in the afternoon, and he offhandedly let me know that this particular party was in its third day and would probably go on for another two. Inside, we shuffled through narrow corridors and pushed aside portable walls. We kept going down, passing through a dank cellar, skipping over what looked like a domestic toilet but was basically a giant hole in the ground. When I asked the same guide why we were going so far below the street level, he laughed and said that unlike the other cities of this world, in Tehran it was the humans, not the rats, who lived underground. Then he opened a door and I understood.

Some nifty entrepreneur had created a replica of a Western-style bar in his house. The bar space itself wasn't very big, but it was surprisingly complete. The walls were painted a tasteful earth color, and the light was dimmed with Chinese paper lanterns. Behind the counter, rows of vodka, rum, gin, and whisky were stacked neatly, as if they'd been lifted from a how-to-run-a-bar manual. The bartender was a tall, attractive young woman with bursts of light freckles on her cheeks who wasted no time telling me how she'd lived in Frankfurt and LA for six years before deciding to move back to Tehran to make some real money. "I was tired of taxes and credit card bills."

"Don't the men here bother you?"

"No more than in LA."

There weren't that many men here right now, anyway. Or women for that matter. I realized it wasn't exactly a party that Nina had sent me to but, for lack of a better word, what I would call an Iranian speakeasy. The liquor was probably bootlegged from Iraq or Turkey or Armenia, or else it came through sailors off the Gulf. Each shot cost roughly the equivalent of $4, which wasn't at all cheap. So the owner—whoever he was—had to easily be making back the money he'd invested in this maze. As for the people who came, maybe they did so out of a dim sense of obligation to live unrestrained lives. But the very existence of this place was a sorry reminder of how restricted their lives really were. This was a controlled environment. It was a virtual world, with real drinks, underneath Tehran. Not a bar, but the simulation of one. I asked the woman behind the counter how often the place was available for "parties" like the one today, and she clamped up. She wouldn't volunteer that sort of information, and knowing how swiftly a place like this might get raided or blackmailed I couldn't blame her.

I looked around. The ambiance reeked of drugs. Everyone appeared exhausted and dulled. When I asked my bartender about this, she shrugged. She had made me a martini in a real martini glass. I had asked for three olives, and she had included those, too. Fat green olives resting in their glass on an artificial counter in a no-name place that was and wasn't a bar. This was what I had meant when I'd tried to explain to Nina why I wanted a party. It was the mystifying sense of a city where the things one saw weren't actually there—not unlike my friend Ziba's feeling when she considered this year's melted snow.

"Why *shouldn't* they be exhausted?" the bartender said. "You would be too if you'd been hanging around for three days."

"Why don't they go home?"

"To do what?"

Sleep, perhaps. Which was what I wanted most just then. A couple of sips of the martini and the jet lag I'd thought I could hold in check for the entire week finally wore me down. There was a heavily made-up woman dancing forlornly to the rhythm of the soft electronic music. I imagined the absurdity of going up to her right at that moment to ask her opinion on a possible American invasion of the country. Perhaps it would have been just as absurd to put the question to the group of scowling young men playing cards at one of the end tables. I looked for my guides but could no longer spot them. A couple in a walled recess had their eyes closed while holding each other's hands. A red bulb shone on their faces, casting a corrupt glare on their momentary innocence.

A fresh batch of customers eventually barged in. They were

a rowdier lot. Well-fed. Wearing expensive clothes. Wealthy kids you'd see any night of winter hanging out at my younger brother's soup-and-sandwich joint by the Dizin ski resort, a half-hour's ride north of Tehran. A girl among them now tried to climb on top of the counter for a dance. But the bartender whispered something in her ear, and the girl reluctantly backed off with a pout.

"What did you tell her?"

"I don't allow it during daytime."

"Why not?"

"Ruins the relaxed mood."

I pointed to the thick red-velvet curtain near the card players and asked her what was on the other side. Private rooms. She suggested I go and sleep off the jet lag I'd been complaining about. In a few hours the place would get busy again, and I'd want to be up for women dancing on the bar.

I wouldn't get to see any bar-top dancing that night, or on any other night of this trip. I'd been stretching out in one of the half-dozen private rooms beyond the red curtain, unable to drift off just yet, feeling ample guilt over the habitual scholarly laziness that kept me from pounding the pavements of Tehran during this short visit. Then a stranger came into the room and coolly told me that we all needed to get out—someone had noticed police activity in the area. Through the maze, then, we all made our way again, but to the surface this time, a mostly hushed line of drained customers probably grateful for a good excuse to go home. Though a male voice did grumble about why the "bar" hadn't paid the local militia enough to avoid this happening. Prohibition-era talk it was—America, circa 1928. I had the rather cinematic notion that the speakeasy might have to camouflage its look for a while. Later, outside the flower shop where they'd originally picked me up, I asked the Peugeot people if I could come back soon. "Talk to lovely Ms. Nina," I was told.

Lovely Ms. Nina would not answer for the next couple of

days. When she finally did, she was crying. Her government man, she said, had been promising her 50 percent ownership of the office he'd bought for their business, and now he'd changed his mind. "I know I shouldn't believe everything I hear in this town." But she always did, and still does. In a way, she and Ziba embodied that dulled energy I'd sensed so vividly in the replicated bar, where the bartender, too, was yet another returnee who lived an underground life in Tehran. Ziba and Nina had come back to Iran to rebuild their lives and half succeeded—in a country where a woman is allowed to inherit half as much property as her brother and where her words in court carry half as much legal weight as a man's.

Women waiting, I thought—with their American passports as backups.

And what they wait for, I imagine, is a combination dream of better days, liberation . . . even invasion. But would they find happiness if the latter came to pass? Or would this happiness be as counterfeit as, say, an eerie barroom below ground or a make-believe democracy thrust upon them, like alms, from above?

Salar Abdoh

is a writer and novelist. He is the author of *The Poet Game.*

Shohreh Aghdashloo

is an actress. She was the first Iranian to be nominated for an Academy Award, in 2003, for her role in *House of Sand and Fog.*

Gelareh Asayesh

is a journalist and writer. She is the author of *Saffron Sky.*

Reza Aslan

is a journalist and writer. He is the author of *No god but God.*

Negar Azimi

works on curatorial projects and is an editor of *Bidoun,* a magazine of contemporary Middle Eastern arts and culture, based in New York.

Babak Ebrahimian

teaches Middle Eastern cinema and literature at Columbia University. He directs theater productions in New York and is the author of *The Cinematic Theater.*

Roya Hakakian

is a journalist and writer. She is the author of *Journey from the Land of No.*

Mehrangiz Kar

is a human rights lawyer and essayist. She was imprisoned in Tehran in 2000 for taking part in a cultural conference held in Berlin on political reform in Iran.

Abbas Kiarostami

is an internationally acclaimed filmmaker. He is the recipient of numerous awards, including the Palme d'Or at Cannes for *Taste of Cherry* in 1997.

Azadeh Moaveni

is a contributing writer to *Time* magazine in Beirut and the author of *Lipstick Jihad.*

Azar Nafisi

is a professor of aesthetics, culture, and literature at the School of Advanced International Studies at Johns Hopkins University and the author of the international bestseller *Reading Lolita in Tehran.*

Shirin Neshat

is a visual artist known for her video installations. Her work has been showcased around the world, most notably at the Whitney Museum of American Art in New York.

Marjane Satrapi

is a graphic artist. Her best-selling comic strip series, *Persepolis,* has won her international recognition.

Daryush Shayegan

is Iran's foremost philosopher. He is the author of numerous books, including *Cultural Schizophrenia* and most recently *Land of Mirages,* an autobiographical narrative.

Naghmeh Zarbafian

is a poet, translator, and independent literary scholar. She is a former student of Azar Nafisi.

ACKNOWLEDGMENTS

My warmest thanks go to Gayatri Patnaik, without whose enthusiasm, intelligence, and sense of humor I would not have undertaken this book. I also wish to thank Alessandra Bastagli, who provided the inspiration, and Larry Weissman, who made it happen.

CREDITS

Babak Ebrahimian: Quoted dialogue from *Where Is the Friend's House?* and *The Wind Will Carry Us* courtesy of Abbas Kiarostami. Omar Khayyam verse excerpted from *Rubaiyat*, in *Khayyam's Quatrains*, selected by Sadegh Hedayat (Tehran, 1923).

Roya Hakakian: Adapted from *Journey from the Land of No* by Roya Hakakian. Copyright © 2004 Roya Hakakian. Used by permission of Crown Publishers, a division of Random House, Inc.

Mehrangiz Kar: Translated from the Persian by Azadeh Pourzand.

Abbas Kiarostami: Translated from the Persian by Lila Azam Zanganeh.

Azar Nafisi: Adapted from a speech given in Rome in June 2004 and an article published in the *Washington Post* on December 6, 2004 ("The Republic of the Imagination"). Copyright © 2004 Azar Nafisi. Reprinted with permission of The Wylie Agency, Inc.

Shirin Neshat: *Fervor*, 2000. Production still. Photo: Larry Barns. Copyright © 2000 Shirin Neshat. Courtesy of Gladstone Gallery, New York. *Tooba*, 2002. Production still. Photo: Larry Barns. Copyright © 2002 Shirin Neshat. Courtesy of Gladstone Gallery, New York.